PUBLIC FINANCE AND ECONOMIC DEVELOPMENT

Spotlight on Jamaica

Hugh N. Dawes

UNIVERSITY
PRESS OF
AMERICA

LANHAM • NEW YORK • LONDON

Copyright © 1982 by

University Press of America,™ Inc.

4720 Boston Way
Lanham, MD 20706

3 Henrietta Street
London WC2E 8LU England

Library of Congress Cataloging in Publication Data

Dawes, Hugh N.
  Public finance and economic development.

  Bibliography: p.
  Includes index.
  1. Jamaica–Economic conditions. 2. Finance, Public
–Jamaica. I. Title.
HC154.D38   338.97292   81–40176
ISBN 0–8191–2091–X
ISBN 0–8191–2092–8 (pbk.)

All University Press of America books are produced on acid-free
paper which exceeds the minimum standards set by the National
Historical Publications and Records Commission.

Dedicated

To Better

Understanding

TABLE OF CONTENTS

List of Tables

List of Tables (Cont'd)

x

LIST OF ILLUSTRATIONS

PREFACE

Economic development requires that there is a high and sustained rate of economic growth. If there was a high rate of growth of the Jamaican economy, this rate of growth has not been sustained. This study aims at illuminating the negative trends which must be arrested if the past vigor in the economy is to be restored. While several aspects of the economy have been examined, the principal focus is on public finance and the extent to which it may be adjusted, refined and used as the main vehicle in the restoration process.

The book is aimed at a wide variety of audiences. First, it could be used as a supplementary text on Public Finance or Economic Development or both largely at the graduate level. But it could also prove useful as a suplementary text to seniors at the undergraduate level where their goals for advanced work in Public Finance and Economic Development have been clearly defined. Secondly, it could be extremely useful to researchers and persons in academia whose specialties are in economics, in general, and public finance or economic development, in particular.

Thirdly, it should be of paramount importance to policy makers and planners of third world emerging countries who are about to make, or in the process of making development plans for the future. One of the many problems of developing countries is that policy makers sometimes plan as though the economies were "closed" when, indeed, they are "open". Specifically, the chapter on Consumption and Foreign Trade will show the indispensability of these variables to development--modified, in the meantime, to suit the computerized age.

Fourthly, persons in quantitative economics or

econometrics could find the manuscript essential as it provides a real world example of how an economy may be modelled and simulated to meet special objectives. In this special respect, it is to be noted, moreover, that the book gives invaluable insights not only on the present status of the economy or the "what is", but also on the future projected goals (to 1985) or the "what ought to be".

Stripped of the technical details, a fifth category of persons will be interested in this book: some for general information; some out of sheer curiosity; and some because of an association, in one way or another, with the country under review. One of the driving forces behind this attraction is the fact that in many ways and for many reasons--including the historic, the strategic, the economic and the political--there is usually a SPOTLIGHT ON JAMAICA. Currently, this spotlight has been shining very bright indeed..

I wish to express my indebtedness to several persons who have helped in the completion of this manuscript. Of the first order, is Professor Bernard Wasow of New York University who gave not only invaluable academic guidance, but also moral encouragement by virture of his warmth and understanding. Sincere thanks are also due to Professors Thomas M. Stanback and James F. Becker, also of New York University who offered many suggestions which proved extremely useful in shaping the final document.

I am also indebted to many person of the technical and academic staff at the Tisch Hall Computer Center of New York University who were very helpful in the computer aspect of the study.

The hard and patient work of the many typists who prepared the drafts is also gratefully acknowledged.

H. N. D.

xiv

CHAPTER 1

INTRODUCTION

The foundations of economics rest on two simple, but, nevertheless, elegant conceptual pillars: "Choice" and "Scarcity". Because of the inherent involvement of scarcity, the point of departure of any economic inquiry presupposes a problem. This is so because since resources are scarce, economic man -- assumed to be a rational creature -- must constantly choose among the various options available to him in a way that he will maximize his satisfaction. The achievement of an economic objective, therefore, is essentially the resolution of a problem or set of problems.

Our discussion begins on what is usually considered a very plausible premise: the idea that no problem can be successfully solved unless it is properly identified. An attempt to answer this identification question is contained in "The Jamaican Problem." A statement and definition of the problem also throw light on the magnitude of the "Task to be Achieved." Once the challenging task ahead is fully appreciated, this will provide the important windows through which the "purpose" and "Significance of this Kind of Investigation" can be readily seen. We conclude Chapter 1 with an "Overview of Research Findings."

THE JAMAICAN PROBLEM

In a very fundamental sense, Jamaica is like all other economies in that it has a limited amount of resources. However, as a developing country, it faces, to a greater or lesser degree, certain problems that are generally characteristic of developing economies as a whole. These include a relatively high illiteracy rate, a comparatively

1

high population increase, a shortage of capital and a shortage of technology. Associating with these broad, general drawbacks, a number of special problems may be cited which have debilitating effects on the growth and health of the Jamaican economy.

First, it is necessary to elaborate on the population issue. While it is true that the population is increasing at a decreasing rate, the current net increase of 1.50 to 1.75 percent per annum is still large enough to offset, in a significant way, the gains that could have been made in the standard of living. Moreover, if the emigration doors are closed to the country, the rate of net increase would approximate 2.41 percent.[1] The population increase is also responsible, in part, for a high unemployment rate of between 20.0 and 25.0 percent.[2]

Second, as will be discussed later, the agricultural industries are not productive enough to supply the domestic needs of the country. Part of this problem is due to inadequate agricultural capital, inadequate arable land, and the changing social attitude of the labor force away from agricultural pursuits. Moreover, agricultural goods for the export market are dependent on the demand and wishes of the developed market economies.

Third, manufacturing and mining, which have been for the last twenty-five years the mainstay of the economy, have been themselves declining during the latter years. One explanation is that the bauxite industry, which features heavily in these two enterprises, has already peaked in terms of investment and production. In addition, bauxite expansion is also taking place in other areas of the world.

---

[1]See National Planning Agency, Economic and Social Survey, Jamaica, 1973 (Kingston: Government publication) p. iii.

[2]Ibid. p. vi.

Fourth, tourism, the nucleus of the service industries, has been quite unstable in recent years. Like bauxite, the tourist business is getting competition from other markets, partly as a result of developments in transportation and communication, including advertising. Sporadic violence which increases risks to both producer and consumer have also had a negative effect.

Fifth, there has been a long-standing adverse trade gap; and, as indicated later, the problem is inclined to remain for some time. In a way, this is not surprising since production is declining and, as hinted earlier, the terms of trade for the primary products are either unfavorable or likely to be.

Sixth, personal saving has been decreasing over the years and this has a restrictive effect on growth. In fact, personal saving is currently negative, supposedly as a consequence of the "demonstration effect" of consumption of developed countries.

Seventh, with the increased bias on consump-tion on the one hand, and the bottlenecks on the other, there have been severe inflationery rates recently. In other words, the "demand pull" and the "cost push" inflation, the two basic types, have been at work in the economy.

Eighth, and as a direct result of the forego-ing, the rate of growth of the economy has been decreasing gradually for some time. The nature of this decline will be examined more critically in the subsequent sections. However, it is important to recognize that the problem evaluation has, in effect, identified a malfunctioning of the primary and secondary industries. Since, there-fore, the tertiary industries are relatively week, the economy as a whole is bound to lose its vitality.

Ninth, superimposed on all the other problems was the uncertainty created after 1972, by the government's experimentation with a new socialist

philosophy referred to as Democratic Socialism.
This problem cannot be overlooked since it obviously had the most precipitous effect on the
economy. If the experiment had merits, it also
carried high risks and uncertainty. As a consequence, there was rapid flight of capital and
technology -- generally regarded as the crucial
ingredients for development -- from an already low
supply. This problem reminds us that the choice
of public policy is not only important but sometimes critical to economic development.

The problems having been identified, general
theory will now be surveyed to see what aspect of
this theory may be brought to bear on the next
important step -- which is an attempt at the
solution of these problems.

TASK TO BE ACHIEVED

This study aims principally at examining
the part public finance -- especially fiscal
policy -- can play in the development of Jamaica.
In so doing, it will endeavor to trace the more
important public financial variables and their
interaction with some of the other significant
facets of the economic system, with a view to
seeing where possible improvement in the development process may be made.

It is assumed in this study that the major
constraint to growth is capital formation. One of
the tasks to be achieved, therefore, will be to
attempt a projection of the capital needs of
the economy to keep its growth at least at its
historical rate for the next five (5) and then
ten (10) years from 1975.[3] Another similar

---

[3]On the question of methodology of these projections, see, for example, Studies in the Long Term Projections for the World Economy: Aggregative Models, United
Nations, New York, 1964; See also, Problems of Long Term
Economic Projections, Development Programming Techniques

objective is to project the capital requirements over the same period of time, assuming the economy grows at some higher rate of growth.

It is self evident that these objectives cannot be satisfactorily achieved unless there is a critical alignment of government's fiscal policy as an indispensable, interdependent component of the overall sources of economic development. Accordingly, a third task to be achieved concerns itself with the general refinements and adjustments that may be made in government's revenue and expenditure policies if the projected targets are to be met.

In the pursuit of these objectives, an attempt will be made to construct and estimate an aggregate macroeconomic model of the Jamaican economy with use of data for the period 1959-1974. Thus the projections to be made, mentioned above, must be further based on the assumption that over the projection period the structure of the economy does not change significantly.

PURPOSE OF THE STUDY

In many a developing country, the problems of economic progress lies not only in scarcity of resources but, more importantly, in how the given resources are used in the production process. While it is true that development plans have been used in Jamaica for some time, most of them tend to be inspired by the ruling political party and are set out as unco-ordinated relationships, merely stating goals and objectives, some of which have no bearing on the ability of the economic system.

Series, No.3, United Nations, New York, 1963; United Nations Conference on Trade and Development (UNCTAD), Trade Prospects and Capital Needs of Developing Countries, United Nations, New York, 1968.

In recent times, a few macroeconomic models have been developed for the Jamaican economy. One type of model is geared merely to explain the general structural behavior of the economy. To the extent that such models throw some light on the probable workings of the economy, they are useful. To the extent, however, that they lack specific objectives in their formulation, they are less informative in terms of a specific package of policies that may be adopted to meet national economic goals. One such model is developed by Carter in his paper, "A Macroeconomic Model for Jamaica, 1959-1966."[4]

The other type of model is more goal oriented. Such models are more efficient and meaningful from the standpoint of a given set of policies that may readily be applied - even if modified - to meet desirable national goals. Perhaps one of the best ones in this category is "Saving and Foreign Trade as Constraints in Economic Growth: A Study of Jamaica," by Harris.[5]

Both of the models described above belong to the genera of models pioneered by Klein and others.[6] The central problem which attends this kind of model building is that since the quantitative estimates are calculated for a past period, once the structure of the economy changes,

[4]Nicholas G. Carter, "A Macro-economic Model of Jamaica, 1959-1966," Social and Economic Studies, (June, 1970), pp. 178-201. Another model which falls into this category is Huntley G. Manhertz, "An exploratory Econometric Model of Jamaica," Social and Economic Studies, (June, 1971), pp. 198-223.

[5]Donald J. Harris, "Savings and Foreign Trade as Constraints in Economic Growth: A Study of Jamaica," Social and Economic Studies, (June, 1970), pp. 147-177.

[6]See, for example, Lawrence R. Klein and A. S. Goldberger, An Economic Model of the United States, 1929-1952 (New York: Humanities Press, 1955).

the predictive value of the model is correspondingly reduced.[7] Accordingly, revision and
updating of these models from time to time is a
necessary prerequisite for future projections for
a developing economy whose structure is likely to
change.

SIGNIFICANCE OF THIS KIND OF INVESTIGATION

     In the period between 1950 and 1965, the
Jamaican economy grew at a rate of 6.5 percent
in real terms. While this overall rate of growth
is relatively impressive, when the rates of
growth are analyzed for different periods of time,
some interesting results emerge. For example,
between 1952 and 1957, the rate of growth averaged
9.7 percent; but between 1958 and 1965, growth
was only 3.6 percent.[8] In the period between
1965 and 1968, growth was only slightly higher
with an average yearly increase of 4.0 percent[9].
Since that time, the indications are that the
average real growth per annum is considerably
smaller.[10].

---

[7]A relatively comprehensive treatment of this matter
is to be found in A. Shourie, The Relevance of Econometric
Models for Medium - and - Longer-Term Projections and Policy
Prescriptions, International Bank of Reconstruction and
Development (IBRD), Department of Economics Working Paper
No. 75, May 1970. For a concise evaluation, see Carter,
op. cit., pp. 178-179.

[8]See Harris, op. cit., pp. 153.

[9]For a fairly extensive evaluation of the declining
rate of growth of the Jamaican economy in recent times, see
Owen Jeffreyson, The Post War Economic Development of Jamaica
(Kingtson: Institute of Social and Economic Research, 1972)
pp. 41-42.

[10]See, for example, National Planning Agency, Economic
and Social Survey of Jamaica, 1973 (Kingston: Government
Publication), pp. 84-87. The Contemporary dramatic increase

7

The above analysis points to the fact that there has been a recent tendency for the rate of expansion of the economy to fall. This study will illuminate some negative trends that must be arrested if the past vigor of the economy is to be restored; and it will suggest alternative public policies that may be adopted toward this end. In particular, the exercise will examine the part the government sector - largely through its taxation and aggregate expenditure - played in the past and the options that are now open to it to help in the restoration and maintenance of desirable rates of growth.

The Carter model was estimated over a relatively short sample period of seven years up to 1965. Moreover, as is expressed above, its emphasis was merely on the structural behavior of the economy; and, therefore, it failed to bring out policy implications. In investigating the role of public finance in the development of Jamaica, modifications of the basic framework of the Carter model will be introduced; and, furthermore, the sample period will be extended over fifteen years from 1959-1974. Hence if the structure of the economy has changed over the recent past, this should be brought out in the analysis in terms of degree and direction.

At the same time, the exercise will also serve to update the Harris model which, although spanning a reasonable sample period of fifteen years, is no longer up-to-date. Here again, this study should give an idea if there are any major structural shifts in the economy within the last ten years.

---

in inflation is indicated on pp. 44-47. Ultimately, the downward trend of economic activity assumed catastrophic proportions. Accordingly, energies currently expended in the administration of the economy must be directed firstly at rehabilitation even before true growth can begin.

AN OVERVIEW OF RESEARCH FINDINGS

The analysis of the role of Public Finance in a developing Jamaica begins on a very fundamental proposition: in every developing country capital, to a greater or lesser degree, is crucial to development and it is in comparatively short supply. Usually capital is in short supply because savings which is the source of capital is low. Saving is low because income is comparatively low and/or consumption is comparatively high. All those activities, therefore, which increase saving directly or indirectly by reducing consumption, add to the potential sources of capital and growth. Naturally, a reversal of this principle has the opposite effect. If, therefore, government the single biggest consumer, reduces its own consumption, increased saving will be available to propel growth. In the same way, where the propensity to consume in the private household is too high, government can use the tax and harness a greater part of the total output in the form of saving to be used for development purposes. Hence, Jamaica's public policy can be so machined as to have significant effects on the growth of the economy.

The chief aim of the study is to investigate the economy of Jamaica so as to shed light on its ability (or inability) to generate the resources necessary for higher rates of growth and a healthier economy. The undertaking is significant since, as discussed above, there has been a secular decline in the growth of the Jamaican economy in real terms, a trend which, if continued, is bound to have very serious consequences for the Jamaican society. The government can play a key role by example and informed economic inducement.

The analytic framework, which centers on a macroeconomic model of the Jamaican economy consisting of fifty-one variables, derives from the proposition that the overall saving of the community is the sum total of the saving of the private sector, the government sector and the

external resource inflow.[11]   Government saving
is at the center of the discussion in line with
the topic under review.   However, this fundamental
principle reminds us that all three sectors need
some amount of investigation before a legitimate
statement can be made about the saving potential
of the country.   The theory further reminds us
that, for any given level of saving, if government
saving goes up, saving in one or the other two
sectors must go down; but the absolute level of
saving can increase if government reduces its
propensity to consume and increases its propensity
to tax.[12]   The latter action has the real effect
of diverting resources from the private sector to
make it available for investment in either the
private sector, the government sector or both.

Saving and investment are equal, ex post.
But investment is also incremental capital,
ultimately yielding the capital stock.   Since the
latter in turn determines national income, the
analytic problem, as it concerns Jamaica, is the
determination of the amount of ex ante saving and
investment necessary to maintain the trend rate of
growth as well as to stimulate higher rates of
growth as required. However, before this type of
determination can be made, it is instructive to
know something not only about the historical
performance of the economy but also the degree to
which the various significant facets of the
economy are interrelated and the type of interrelationships.

The statistical analyses are quite revealing.   Chapter 3 contains the functions having to
do with consumption and foreign trade.   Unlike

---

[11]See equation (3), Chapter 2.

[12]For an appreciation of the possible quantitative
effect of such an increased propensity to tax see Evans,
op. cit., pp. 543-594.   See also Bowers and Baird op. cit.,
pp. 47-58. However, these variables should be given opposite
signs since they are describing developing economies.

10

the finding of some recent researchers, this
investigation suggests that personal consumption
follows standard empirical behavior and relates to
current disposable income as well as previous
income and consumption patterns in line with the
well known "permanent income hypothesis". However,
there is a clear indication of a marginal propensity to consume greater than one (1) and this has
been creating an extraordinary pressure on the
overall resources for growth. Government consumption depends on net revenues collected and total
economic activity. Moreover, according to the
derived elasticity index, the rate of government
purchases seems to keep very close to the rate
of the overall output produced. In the foreign
trade sector, exports of goods are treated exogenously since they usually depend on weather
conditions or the wishes and demands of the
developed economies. Exports of services, however, are found to vary directly with gross
domestic product and inversely with the accumulated fixed investment.

Imports are categorized under appropriate
subdivisions and their functions shown in Table 4.
The highlights are worth emphasizing. Food
and non-food, or consumer imports, have been
declining not because of increased domestic
production but, apparently, because of policy
to encourage more private saving and a healthier
balance of payments position. Capital imports
are indispensable to the country since on the
margin more than one-half of the equipment for
fixed investment originates abroad. So too are
the imports of intermediate goods which accounted
for 42.0 percent of all imports in 1974.

As indicated earlier, government revenue is
inextricably linked with development since overall
saving consists, in part, of government saving
which in turn depends on net government revenues
collected. It follows, therefore, that the size
of the saving-investment gap depends to a great
extent on government's tax effort. Chapter 4
concerns the analysis of the government revenue
and its implication for economic development. The

11

various instruments of revenue and their behavior are presented in Table 5 (page 52) and, immediately, convey the idea that it is the relative rather than the absolute yield of the instruments which is important since different taxes will have different degrees of impact on output.

Indirect taxes, including excises (Te), custom duties (Tc), and other indirect taxes (Toi) account for approximately 42.0 percent of all revenues in 1974. Of this total, other indirect taxes generate about one-half. The elasticity index of 2.054 (not shown in Table 5) relative to gross domestic product underscores the importance of this group of taxes as earners of government income. Incidentally, the elasticity indices of this study are calculated either at the point of means or, as in the case of the sectorial elasticities of chapter 2, by the use of double log functions where the exponents represent the elasticities directly.

Direct taxes, comprising business and personal income taxes, were responsible for about 66.0 percent of net revenues collected in 1974.[13] This is a dramatic change from their position in 1965 when they generated 46.5 percent.

Of the direct taxes, the business tax showed the more rapid rate of growth over the last decade, increasing from 26.0 percent in 1965 to 42.6 percent of net revenues in 1974, as a direct result of tax reform, review of the tax holidays and, particularly, review of bauxite taxes. Personal income taxes with an elasticity on personal income of 3.379 have a high growth potential, especially as the tax system is a

---

[13]If the sum of direct and indirect taxes appears to be more than 100.00 percent, it is because in the calculation of net revenues, subsidies and other minor transfers from government assume negative values. These, when added to the total, will reduce the final figure to 100.00 percent.

progressive one. Nor does it appear that the current rate of this tax is such as to cause any serious negative feedback on labor supply in the immediate future.

Local transfers from government should not only be based on political philosophy but also on economic considerations, especially since the recipients usully have a very high marginal propensity to consume. A similar care should be taken in making subsidies which may be misappropriated from production to consumption, given unnecessarily (for example, some tax holidays under the Industrial Incentive Laws), or which would fail to create the desired effect.

The real impact of external transfers to and from the government is less clear (more will be said about these later); although, superficially, it is reasonable to assume that most incoming gifts to the government are favorable to the development process. Current government external transfer payments, largely oriented to international organizations, should be limited to the level commensurate with an informed judgment of their estimated benefits.

For purposes of this study, total saving is analyzed as personal saving, business saving, government saving, saving from depreciation and net foreign borrowing. Saving is partly the subject of Chapter 5 and the various functions are shown in Table 6 (page 69). An important feature of saving in Jamaica is the fact that personal saving is a negative quantity because the marginal propensity to consume is greater than one (1). This may be due to the demonstration effect of consumption in nearby America as well as expected [14] "permanent" income from bauxite and tourism.

---

[14] For a reference to the "permanent income hypothesis" of consumption, see Chapter 2. It should be ob-

13

The distribution of saving among the various categories based on 1974 figures is also shown in Table 6. It merits more than passing interest that government saving was the largest category while business saving was third in line. If business or personal saving is expatriated and/or diverted to expensive housing, this could cause real problems for development. Since the country can only grow within the limits dictated by total saving, borrowing from abroad is an absolute necessity, especially at a time when national income is undergoing a decreasing trend.

The investment and production functions are set out in Table 7. Fixed investment is divided into the private and public sectors with an approximate 85.0 to 15.0 percent share, respectively. The public share is funded by using 18 cents of every dollar of net revenues generated. As regards production, while total output depends on the capital stock, the core of the industrial sector, consisting of manufacturing, mining, construction, transportation and utilities (Y5s) is explainable by total output. The relationship suggests, moreover, that about 48.0 percent or nearly one-half of economic growth occurs in the industrial sector as the term is crudely defined here.

The ultimate goal of the study involves the projections of different sets of resource allocation which are consistent with alternative rates of growth of output. However, before this is attempted, various verification tests, including a simulation of the economy will be undertaken to ascertain the reliability of the model. These verification indices which are generally within standard accepted limits are, in fact, shown in Table 8 (page 85).

---

served, too, that tourists from developed economies with high consumption patterns could also help to aggravate the demonstration effect syndrome.

The solution of the system involves the use of the observed values of the predetermined variables of 1974 in accordance with certain stated assumptions found on page 90, regarding their future growth. Given these observed values and accompanying assumptions, a unique solution of the entire system presents itself as the system is projected forward. The solution exercise is the subject of Appendix A.

Table 9 (page 91) presents the values of national income aggregates and the government sector for 1975 and projects them to 1985 assuming that only the historical trend rate of growth is guaranteed. The figures indicate a relative increase in government activity as income increases. The trend rate also necessitates increased total saving and investment of 20.6 percent by 1980 and 45.7 percent by 1985; or, alternatively, investment must continue to assume about 23.6 percent of GNP annually.

The values of the resources necessary to achieve alternative rates of growth in the short run between 1975 and 1980 are shown in Table 10 (page 97). The associated values that other key variables will assume are also listed. Table 11 (page 102) presents the corresponding long-run figures between 1981 and 1985.

The figures of both tables reveal that to get higher rates of growth, sacrifice in the form of reduced consumption must be made to allow for more saving and investment. However, in the long run, income will be so high, comparatively, that even if a higher proportion is set aside for saving the standard of living will still increase significantly over the situation existing in 1975.

CHAPTER 2

S O L V I N G   T H E   P R O B L E M:
R E S E A R C H   M E T H O D O L O G Y

THE MEANING OF ECONOMIC DEVELOPMENT

Because matter cannot be created (or de-
stroyed), economic growth must necessarily be ac-
companied by costs and sacrifices--at least in the
initial stages. These sacrifices usually take the
form of the present consumption which must be
foregone so that more resources can be saved for
producer goods production. It is because of the
associating costs why W. A. Lewis is ambivalent
about the efficacy of economic growth.[1]

Sometimes the terms "economic growth" and
"economic development" are used interchangeably;
and this is generally acceptable. However, a useful distinction is sometimes drawn between the two
concepts, although one usually implies the other.
Kindleberger, for example, maintains that economic
growth merely means "more output", and economic
development implies more output as well as changes
in the technical and institutional arrangements by
which this output is produced.[2] In this view,

---

[1] See his "Is Economic Growth Desirable?" in his
Theory of Economic Growth (New York: Richard D. Irwin,
1955). This text is sometimes regarded as a modern classic
on the subject of economic growth and development. This
section of the book is reprinted in Development and Society:
The Dynamics of Economic Change, ed. by David E. Novack and
Robert Lekachman (New York: St. Martin's Press, 1968, P.
10-22.

[2] Charles P. Kindleberger, Economic Development (2nd
ed.; New York: McGraw Hill, 1965), p. 1.

growth without development is meaningless, as would be the case, for example, if Brazil were to produce more and more coffee.

Some countries which have achieved a significant degree of growth find it difficult not only to continue to grow but to maintain the level of growth already attained. Economic development is concerned with rapid as well as sustained rates of economic growth. To this extent, all countries are unavoidably interested in the subject.

TWO THEORIES OF ECONOMIC GROWTH

Although there are various types of growth models, including the so-called "stage-models",[3] contemporary growth theory revolves largely around two basic types: the Harrod-Domar[4] model and the newer, neoclassical models, developed around aggregate production functions. The following discussion is intended to give a brief appraisal of their central features rather than to describe the large varieties which may be encountered.

In the Harrod-Domar model, growth results from a constant capital-output ratio and the marginal propensity to save, with capital as the primary stimulating force causing growth. In algebraic symbols:

---

[3] For one of the most popular of these models, see W. W. Rostow, The Stages of Economic Growth (Cambridge: Cambridge University Press, 1960).

[4] For Harrod's contribution see R. F. Harrod, Towards a Dynamic Economics (New York: St. Martin's Press, 1948). For Domar's contribution see E. D. Domar, "Capital Expansion, Rate of Growth and Employment", Econometrica (April, 1946), pp. 137-147.

S/Y = saving ratio(s); dK/dY = incremental capital-output ratio (k)

$$\text{Since } S = I, \ S/Y = I/Y. \quad \text{But}$$
$$\text{growth} \quad (G) = dY/Y = \frac{I/Y}{I/dY} = \frac{s}{k}$$

The above expression states that growth is equal to the saving ratio, divided by the marginal or incremental capital-output ratio. Constancy of the capital-output ratio, it should be noted, requires that it is equal to the incremental capital-output ratio.

Since investment increases both supply capacity and aggregate demand, the problem of the Harrod-Domar model is to find an equilibrium growth path such that the increase of the potential output is consistent with the increased aggregate demand generated. To illustrate this, let

Q = output

Y = aggregate demand. Then

Y = C + I = Q

C = aY (long-run consumption function)

Y = 1/ (1-a) I where

1/ (1-a) is the investment multiplier (m)

Y = mI = Q

dY = mdI = dQ

Dividing these last two equations give

dY/y = dI/I = dQ/Q

The last equation gives the "warranted"rate of growth of investment and the emergence of a "steady state" economic growth where investment, the capital stock, output, saving and consumption are all growing at the same rate. The "natural

18

rate" of growth, which is the rate of growth of the labor force will, however, influence the capital-output ratio through diminishing returns until it is equivalent to the warranted rate. This implies that in the long run only technological advance can increase per capita income.

In spite of the usefulness of the Harrod-Domar model, it has some shortcomings. First, by concentrating only on capital, it presupposes a capital theory of value. Labor can only feature in the system at a constant capital-labor ratio and this is realistic only if capital and labor grow at the same rate, or if labor is continuously redundant. Second, it ignores the possibility of technological progress. Third, any growth of investment above or below the warranted rate will cause, through the "acceleration principle," uncontrollable inflation and incurable depression, respectively. Fourth, empirically, growth tends to proceed faster than can be explained by capital inputs with a constant capital-output ratio.[5]

The shortcomings mentioned above led to the investigation of neoclassical models which allowed for flexible capital-output ratios and substitution of capital for labor.[6] In these models, aggregate demand is not considered and the assumption is that output, expressed by the aggregate production function, depends on the amount of the factor inputs used. Accordingly, the production

[5] See for example, M. Abromovitz, "Resource and Output Trends in the United States Since 1870," American Economic Review Proceedings, May 1956, pp. 5-23. See also Robert Solow "Technical Change and the Aggregate Production Function," Review of Economics and Statistics, August 1957, pp. 312-320.

[6] One of the pioneers in this area is Robert Solow. See his "Contribution to the Theory of Economic Growth," Quarterly Journal of Economics, (February, 1956), pp. 65-94.

function can be expressed as

$$Q = f(K, L, T(t))$$

where Q is output; K is capital; L is Labor; T is technology which, itself, is a function of time, t.

If the assumption of technological change is relaxed

$$Q = f (K, L)$$

$$dQ = dQ/dK. \quad dK + dQ/dL. \quad dL = 0$$

The above expression, implying constant return to scale, states that change in income is the sum of the marginal product of capital times the increase in capital and the marginal product of labor times the increase in labor. The expression also states that if the total output is held constant

$$- \frac{dL}{dK} = \frac{dQ/dK}{dQ/dL}$$

This suggests that the marginal rate of substitution (MRS) of labor for capital is equal to the ratio of their marginal products.

The exact way in which technology enters the production process is still controversial. However, it is generally agreed that it is either incorporated in the embodied form as a result of a more productive form of labor and/or capital; or through the disembodied form due to the development of new and different combinations of labor and capital.

How can this survey of development theory help to solve the problems mentioned in the first chapter? What, in fact, is at stake? What must be done? The answers to these questions are contained in the following sections.

BASIC FRAMEWORK EMPLOYED

Capital needs of an economy may be generated via the link between saving and investment. The framework for the analysis of the saving-investment required may be set out by making use of the well-known national income identities:

(1) $Y = C + I + G + X - M$

(2) $Y = C + Spr + Rn$

Where Y = Total Product

        C = Private consumption

        I = Gross investment

        G = Government consumption

        X = Export

        M = Imports

      Spr = Private saving

      Rn = Net government revenue

The first equation defines total income in terms of expenditure flow; while equation (2) describes it from the standpoint of how this income is allocated. From equation (1) and (2) we have:

(3) $I = Spr + (Rn - G) + (M - X)$

Equation (3) states that the sum of private saving, government saving, and foreign saving (including net borrowing or lending) is equivalent to

21

gross investment. This is true in the ex post or
accounting sense. If this were also true in the
ex ante sense, then equation (3) would also cha-
racterize the basic condition necessary for the
system to achieve equilibrium.

Especially pertinent to the study, equation
(3) thus highlights some of the major aggregates
in the form of the flow of local and foreign resources which are particularly relevant to growth
in a developing economy.[7] An analytic problem,
therefore, concerns the policies to be employed in
the process of adjusting planned saving to planned
investment, given a plan and rate of development.
The capital stock, K_t, in the system may be given

---

[7] In equation (3), foreign and domestic saving are
full substitutes. Many macroeconomic models of less developed countries emphasize that external saving not only
fills a saving-investment gap, but that it also fills an
import-export gap. These two gaps can be unequal, ex ante,
and thus external saving can be different in its impact on
growth than is domestic saving. Our model focuses on the
investment requirements for targeted growth rates. As we
will see in chapter 5, however, the foreign exchange gap
will be evident in extremely low imports of non-food and
general consumer goods--the residual category. Two-gap approaches to macroeconomic projection can be explored in H.
B. Chenery and A. M. Strout, "Foreign Assistance and Economic Development", American Economic Review, September 1966.
See also UNCTAD. Trade Prospects, op. cit. Other authorities argue that these discreet so-called gaps can only exist
in the absence of proper socio-economic and allocation policies by policy makers. See, for example, H. J. Burton, "The
Two-Gap Approach to Development: Comment", American Economic
Review, June 1969, pp. 439-446. In this study, the focus
will not be on the two gaps as such but on any disparity
between desired saving and desired investment, regardless of
its source.

at any time, t, by the sum of the initial capital stock, Ko, and the accumulation of net investment of the form:[8]

$$(4) \qquad Kt \quad = \quad Ko + (1-d) \sum_{1=0}^{n-1} Ifi$$

where d is assumed to be a constant and refers to depreciation of total fixed capital formation at time t. The overall production function may be set out behaviorally as a proportional relationship between capital and output thus:

$$(5) \qquad Yt \quad = \quad kKt$$

where k is a constant and is the inverse of the capital coefficient or capital output ratio. Equations (4) and (5) give

$$(6) \qquad Yt \quad = \quad kKo + k(1-d) \sum_{i=0}^{n-1} Ifi$$

The rest of the model is summarized for convenience below. However, a brief description follows on pages 24, 25 and 26.

THE MODEL

I. <u>Consumption</u> (personal)

$$(1) \quad C \quad = \quad c_o + c_1 Yd + C_2 C_t{-1}$$

---

[8] Although a perpetual inventory method may have advantages over this method of estimating capital, the assessment of capital accumulation in this manner has been successfully accomplished by some authorities. See, for example, United Nations, <u>Studies in Long Term Projections</u> op, cit. pp. 56–62; United Nations, <u>Problems of Long Term Economic Projections</u>, op. cit. p. 11; Harris, op. cit., p. 150.

II. <u>Government</u> (consumption)

$$G \quad = \quad g_0 + g_1 R_n + g_2 Y$$

III. <u>Foreign Trade</u>

(a) Exports

(1) $X_g \quad = \quad X_{go}$ (Exogenous)

(2) $X_s \quad = \quad X_{so} + Xs_1 Y + Xs_2 \sum_{i=o}^{n} Ifi$

(b) <u>Imports</u>

(1) $Mf \quad = \quad mf_o + mf_1 Yd$

(2) $Mnf \quad = \quad mnf_o + Mnf_1 Mc + mnf_2 Pop$

(3) $Mk \quad = \quad mk_o + mk_1 If$

(4) $Mig \quad = \quad mig_o + mig_1 Y_5 s$

(5) $Mfs \quad = \quad mfs_o + mfs_1 Mk + mfs_2 D_1$

(6) $Mos \quad = \quad mos_o + mos_1 Y$

IV. <u>Government Sector</u> (Revenue)

(1) $Tc \quad = \quad tc_o + tc_1 Y_5 s + Tc_2 ETus$

(2) $Te \quad = \quad te_o + te_1 Y_5 s$

(3) $Toi \quad = \quad toi_o + toi_1 Y$

(4) $Tyg \quad = \quad tyg_o + tyg_1 Y + Tyg_2 Trg$

(5) $Tb \quad = \quad tb_o + tb_1 \ 11$

(6) $Tpy \quad = \quad tpy_o = tpy_1 Y_p$

(7) $Trp \quad = \quad trp_o$ (Exogenous)

24

$$(8) \quad Trg = trg_0 \text{ (Exogenous)}$$

$$(9) \quad Trxg = trxg_0 \text{ (Exogenous)}$$

$$(10) \quad Trmg = trmg_0 \text{ (Exogenous)}$$

$$(11) \quad Tsu = tsu_0 + tsu_1 Y$$

V. Saving

(1) Sg i.e.   (Rn–G) Residual from equation 11 (1)

(2) Sp i.e.   (Yd–C) Residual from equation 1 (1)

$$(3) \quad Sb = sb_0 + sb_1 \widehat{11}$$

$$(4) \quad \widehat{11} = \widehat{11}_0 + \widehat{11}_1 Yn$$

$$(5) \quad Sd = sd_0 + sd_1 \sum_{i=0}^{n} Ifi$$

$$(6) \quad Smnb = smnb_0 \text{ (Exogenous)}$$

VI. Investment and Production

$$(1) \quad Yt = kK_0 + k(1-d) \sum_{i=0}^{n-1} Ifi$$

$$(2) \quad Y_{5s} = Y5s_0 + y5s_1 Y$$

$$(3) \quad In = in_0 \text{ (Exogenous)}$$

$$(4) \quad If_g = ifg_0 + ifg_1 Rn$$

VII. Identities

$$(1) \quad M = C + I + G + X + Mfs - Y - Xfs$$

$$(2) \quad Mc = M - Mk - Mig - Mos - Mfs$$

$$(3) \quad Rn = Tc + Te + Toi + Tyg + Tb + Typ - Trp + Trg + Trxg - Trmg - Tsu$$

25

$$(4) \quad S \quad = \quad Sg + Sp + Sb + Sd + Smnb$$

$$(5) \quad Sg \quad = \quad Rn - G$$

$$(6) \quad Sp \quad = \quad Yd - C - Trg - Trmp$$

$$(7) \quad X \quad = \quad Xg + Xs$$

$$(8) \quad If \quad = \quad Ifg + Ifpr$$

$$(9) \quad I \quad = \quad If + In$$

$$(10) \quad Yd \quad = \quad Yp - Tpy$$

$$(11) \quad Yp \quad = \quad Yn - Tb - Tyg - Sb + Trp$$

$$(12) \quad Yn \quad = \quad Y + Xfs - Mfs - Sd - (Tc + Te + Toi) + Tsu$$

$$(13) \quad Ifpr \quad = \quad S - In - Ifg$$

CATALOGUE OF VARIABLES

C	= private consumption
D_1	= dummy (1959 - 67 = 0, 1968 - 74 = 1.00)
ETus	= Expenditure on travel, U.S.A.
G	= Government consumption
$\sum_{i=o}^{n-1} If_i$	= accumulated investment lagged one (1) year
$\sum_{i=o}^{n} If_i$	= accumulated investment
I	= gross investment
If	= fixed investment
Ifg	= fixed government investment
Ifpr	= fixed private investment
In	= inventory investment/(changes in stock)

26

Ko	=	capital stock (1959 = 0)
Kt	=	capital stock at time, t.
M	=	import of goods and services
Mc	=	import of consumer goods
Mf	=	import of food
Mnf	=	import of non-food
Mk	=	import of capital goods
Mig	=	import of intermediate goods
Mfs	=	payment for factor services
Mos	=	payment for other services
Pop	=	population
Π	=	profits
Rn	=	net government revenue
S	=	saving
Sg	=	Government saving
Sp	=	personal saving
Sig	=	saving - investment gap
Sb	=	business saving
Sd	=	saving from depreciation
Smnb	=	saving from net foreign borrowing
Tc	=	customs duties
Te	=	excise taxes
Tyg	=	income from government enterprises

Toi	=	other indirect taxes
Tb	=	business taxes
Typ	=	personal income taxes
Trp	=	transfer from government to persons
Trg	=	transfer from private sector to government
Trxp	=	foreign transfer receipts by the private sector
Trmp	=	foreign transfer payments by the private sector
Trxg	=	foreign transfer receipts by the government
Trmg	=	foreign transfer payments by the government
Tsu	=	subsidies
X	=	export of goods and services
Xg	=	exports of goods
Xs	=	exports of services
Xfs	=	receipts of factor services
Y	=	total output
Yd	=	personal disposable income
Y5s	=	output of five sectors: mining, manufacturing, construction, transportation, and utilities.
Yn	=	national income
Yp	=	personal income

Consumption is divided into personal and government, the latter representing the recurrent expenditure of the public sector and is made a

28

function of public revenue and total economic activity. In the foreign trade sector, merchandise
export is made completely exogenous considering
that, by and large, the demand for the goods ex-
ported depends on the needs of world markets, the
needs of Jamaica's trading partners, and even the
international political climate. Furthermore, the
export crops and their products are subject to the
vagaries of the weather. Export of services is,
however, endogenous depending on gross output and
accumulated capital. Imports are made endogenous
to the system and are divided essentially into
consumer and capital goods. Another broad category which could be called "miscellaneous imports"
includes items like payments for factor services.

The government sector (revenue) is particularly highly disaggregated as this is the focus of
the study. One can, however, discern broad categories such as direct and indirect taxes, government enterprise income, transfers and subsidies.
All these categories except transfers are endogenous to the system. The decision to leave transfers exogenous can be defended on the grounds
that, at least in part, they depend on the political wishes and actions of the government concerned.

Saving is on the whole expressed by individual
saving function for both the private and public
sectors, sometimes as residuals from corresponding
consumption functions. Net foreign borrowing is,
however, left exogenous since it will depend to a
large degree on subjective entrepreneurial skills
as well as the political stability of the country.

Part of the investment and production functions have already been described in introducing
the model. Five sectors (Y5s), manufacturing,
mining, construction, transportation, and utilities representing a cross section of the industrial sector is explained in relation to gross
domestic product; and public investment is assumed
to be a function of revenues collected.

To facilitate easy interpretation of the
model, a list of variables and their full descrip-

tion is provided on pages 26, 27, and 28.

ECONOMIC REVIEW: AN HISTORICAL PERSPECTIVE

The data for the period under review reveals that the compound growth rate for the real gross domestic product at market prices for the period 1959-66 was 4.1 percent. This contrasts sharply with a growth rate of only 2.5 percent for the period 1967-74, confirming the observation made earlier that the growth of the economy has a strong tendency to decrease over time. The growth rate for the overall period was a modest 3.7 percent.

Exports of goods and services made a reasonable contribution to this modest growth over the period, moving from 34.2 percent of gross domestic product in 1959 to 41.5 percent in 1974. During the same time, imports rose from 42.5 to 48.0 percent of gross domestic product. While, therefore, there is a somewhat greater proportionate gain in exports than imports, the gap between the two remains essentially the same and, as to be expected, continues to cause the chronic problem of financing the trade gap.

The deficits were financed largely by the inflow of foreign capital. This capital inflow contributed considerably at the same time to the level of gross investment. In 1968, for example, the ratio of foreign capital to gross investment expressed in real terms was as high as 56.0 percent; the overall average for the period was 26.0 percent. This is, of course, in turn reflected in an ever increasing rise in the payments to factor services.[9]

---

[9] Although foreign capital is an important source of investment, it is not without its complications. For an idea of some of the possible complexities, see Jeffreyson, op. cit, Chapter 9. For the real issues of a more critical import see especially pp. 247-249. See also Albert O. Hirschman, "How to divest in Latin America and Why", Essays In International Finance No. 76, November, Princeton University; Charles Kennedy, "Keynesian Theory in an Open Economy", Social and Economic Studies Vol. 15, March, 1966.

COMPARATIVE SECTORIAL PERFORMANCE

Table 1 is quite revealing. It sets out the elasticities and compound growth rates at factor cost by sectors and gives a good indication as to the relative degree of sector viability and responsiveness to growth.

Moreover, the table shows some of the basic structural shifts that have taken place over the past ten years compared with what existed for the fifteen-year period previously.[10]

Interestingly, over the twenty-five-year period, the sector, Mining Quarrying and Refining as well as those of Utilities and Finance maintained their rank positions of first, second and third respectively, with respect to their compound growth rates and their elasticities. However, over the past ten years the buoyancy of the Mining and Utilities sectors have been significantly dampened. Whereas, over the previous fifteen year period, their elasticities were respectively 2.927 and 2.041, over the past ten year period they were only 1.875 and 1.522. This is reflected in their growth rates which were 14.7 and 11.2 percent in the previous period but only 10.9 and 10.1 percent in the last period.

On the extreme end of the scale, although agriculture shows some improvement over the last period, it continues to be very inelastic and only places above Ownership of Dwellings with respect to the trend in growth. As one of the more vital sectors in a developing economy, the alarm over the performance of this sector is understandable.

---

[10] Figures for this period are adopted from Harris, op. cit, p. 152. The trend in some of these structural shifts is also well captured in Jeffreyson, op. cit.

Table 1

Sectorial Growth Elasticities and Growth Rates

Sectors	Elasticities on GDP (F.C.)[a]		Compound Growth Rate	
	1950-65	1965-74	1950-65	1965-74
Agriculture, Forestry & Fishing	0.056	0.327	0.005	0.020
Mining, Quarrying & Refining	2.927	1.875	0.147	0.109
Manufacture,	1.134	0.850	0.063	0.053
Construction & Installation	1.232	0.564	0.058	0.037
Electricity, Gas, and Water	2.041	1.522	0.112	0.101
Transportation, Storage, and Communication	1.210	1.313	0.066	0.087
Distributive Trade	0.814	1.088	0.041	0.054
Financial Institutions	1.363	1.386	0.064	0.091
Ownership of Dwellings	0.362	0.0676	0.023	0.005
Public Administration	1.184	1.140	0.065	0.080
Miscellaneous Services	0.988	0.939	0.055	0.060
GDP (F.C.)	--	--	0.053	0.053

a   GDP (F.C.) refers to gross domestic product at
factor cost. The growth rate of GDP (F.C.) is the
same both for the recent and the early period presumably because the historical maximum growth rate
occurred between 1964 and 1965, the dividing line
separating both periods.

Two other sectors, Manufacturing and Construction, need special attention. These sectors were elastic in the first period, but inelastic in the second. The relative decline of Construction and Installation can possibly be explained by the slowdown of growth in the bauxite industry.[11] At this stage of Jamaica's development, a reasonable case can be made for the desirability of the manufacturing sector to grow at least as fast as the overall economy. Accordingly, this is one of the sectors to which attention should be urgently turned.[12]

ANALYSIS OF IMPORTANT MACROECONOMIC RATIOS

Various self-explanatory aggregative indices of historical performance are carried in Table

---

[11] This possibility has been alluded to in recent times. See, for example, National Planning Agency, Economic and Social Survey of Jamaica, 1970, page 9.

[12] One important view of Economic Development is that development is concomitant with a shift from primary to secondary to tertiary industries. For a concise analysis of this theory, see Colin Clarke, The Conditions of Economic Progress (2nd edn.; London: Macmillan, 1951), p. 401. Since Jamaica is not regarded as a developed economy, it cannot by this theory, be in the tertiary stage where the predominant service industries are presumably predicated on a reasonably strong primary and/or secondary sector. By simple logic, therefore, this theory presupposes that manufacturing which is a most important part of the secondary stage should be at least as viable as the overall economy and preferably much more so if the ultimate tertiary stage is to be comfortably conquered.

Table 2

HISTORICAL STRUCTURE AND PERFORMANCE

General Index	Quantitative Index		Median of 31 Developing Countries
	1950-65	1959-74[a]	
Ratio of Gross National Saving/(GNP)	0.16	0.16	0.12
Ratio of net Foreign Capital Inflow/GNP	0.04	0.06	0.04
Ratio of Gross Domestic Investment/GNP	0.20	0.212	0.17
Ratio of Imports of Goods and Services/GNP	0.34	0.446	0.20
Marginal National Saving Ratio	0.23	0.254	0.19
Incremental Capital-Output Ratio	2.23	3.704	3.52
Marginal Import Ratio	0.41	0.303	0.20
Growth Rate of Gross Investment	0.07	0.057	0.07
Growth Rate of Exports of Goods and Services	0.107	0.040	0.051
Growth Rate of GNP	0.062	0.037	0.046

[a]

Estimated by fitting time trend to actual observations. A very slight statistical discrepancy exists between gross saving and gross investment but this is attributed to problems of aggregation and rounding errors.

2.[13]   The average national Saving and average
Investment remained roughly the same over the past
quarter century but there was a significant increase in capital inflow over the last ten-year
period.   It should be observed, too, that unlike
the first period, the marginal import ratio is
less than the average for the last ten years, suggesting a relative decline in the comparative
amount of goods and services that are likely to be
imported in the immediate period following 1974.

It is noteworthy that during the last period
both the growth rates of exports and GNP fell
sharply and this obviously has some bearing on the
falling off of the growth of investment from 7.0
to 5.7 percent.   Since these figures fell below
the median for the representative sample of developing countries, one can argue with further justification that better planning and productivity
is called for in the economy.   One consolation,
however, lies in the fact that the marginal national saving ratio is well above the average,
indicating a rising average and hence a potential
increase in one of the major sources of growth.

---

[13]   The estimation technique used in computing these
indices is that of fitting time trend to actual observations.   For a good appreciation as to how Jamaica's economy
performed in the past compared with what is likely to obtain
in other developing countries, see Harris, op. cit, p. 153
from which the figures in the first period (1950-65) are
taken.   One is invited, particularly, to observe the figures
representing the median indices of thirty-one developing
countries since they represent a useful barometer of expected performance.   For a more comprehensive account of
these indices, see also H. B. Chenery and A. M. Strout,
"Foreign Assistance and Economic Development", American
Economic Review, September, 1966, pp. 682-84.

CHAPTER 3

C O N S U M P T I O N   A N D   F O R E I G N   T R A D E

Chapter 3 presents the statistical analysis as well as the discussion of consumption and Foreign Trade transactions. The revelations of this chapter are crucial to the study because on the one hand, the amount of consumption under- taken will indicate how much remains for saving and eventually investment. The latter will form what is usually considered as the primary engine of growth in a developing economy. On the other hand, the foreign trade sector will indicate not only the role of additional saving and capital from abroad, but will also detail the structure of exports and imports within the economy.

STATISTICAL ESTIMATION

The results of the overall statistical analysis are described in this section. The choice among different relationships of an equation is determined by economic theory, peculiar Jamaican conditions, the coefficient of determination, R^2, The Durbin-Watson statis- tic, d, and the "t" statistic, t.

The value of the t statistic represents the ratio of the estimated parameter and its standard error and is found within parentheses immediately under each parameter.

Table 3 presents the quantitative values of personal and government consumption and, as is the case throughout the study, linear relationships are assumed. The assessment of these values is the subject of the discussion immediately follow- ing this section. In view of the sample size and the fact that many of the equation are simple relationships, the estimation technique used is ordinary least squares (OLS) whose efficiency is expected to compare favorably with other techniques under these conditions.[1]

Before we proceed to analyze the various components of consumption and trade, let us present the basic statistical results. As mentioned before, the explantation will follow.

The only part of exports which is put in a stochastic relationship is the service sector. The specification is shown below:

$$Xs = -85.8180 + 0.3288y - 0.0338 \text{ Ifi} \sum_{i=o}^{n}$$
$$(-2.6729) \quad (4.7432) \quad (-2.7432)$$

$$R^2 = 0.881 \qquad\qquad d = 1.202$$

TABLE 3

Quantitative and Statistical Values
of Consumption

Dependent Variable	% Of Consumption 1974	Parameters		Independent Variable	R^2	d
		Constant	Coefficient			
C	80.6	-39.3281 (1.3986)	0.7081 (4.1733)	Yd	0.968	
			0.3675 (2.5035)	C_{t-1}		
G	19.4	-32.4364 (-3.0273)	0.3368 (4.0672)	R_n	0.966	1.292
			0.1171 (4.2529)	Y		

---

[1]M. Dutta and V. Su arrived at some conclusive findings on this point. See their "An Economic Model of Puerto Rico", Review of Economic Studies, Vol XXXVI, No. 107 (July 1969) p. 321. See also Harris, op.cit., p. 150 and Manherts, op. cit., p. 201 for general agreement on the matter.

The functions and estimates for imports are contained in the table which follows. These estimates will be evaluated under their appropriate caption later in the chapter.

TABLE 4

Functions and Indices of Imports

De-pendent Variable	% Of Imports 1974	Parameters		Independent Variable	R^2	d
		Constant	Coefficient			
Mf	11.7	4.59507 (0.8382)	0.0662 (5.3762)	Yd	0.674	1.2967
Mnf	9.2	38.9014 (4.4915)	0.8086 (11.8461) 0.3147 (-7.9440)	Mc Pop	0.935	0.8286
Mk	20.4	4.63636 (0.4131)	0.5342 (6.3283)	If	0.741	1.9313
Mig	42.0	-114.429 (-6.2643)	0.6993 (10.0748)	Y5s	0.879	0.4835
Mfs	7.7	-5.27262 (-0.5324)	1.0011 (4.6316) -41.6424 -4.0298	Mk D_1	0.627	2.0538
Mos	9.0	15.0058 (4.2169)	0.0277 (4.9102)	Y	0.633	1.2841

38

Some researchers who have studied the Jamaican consumption function in recent times have found that it needed special treatment if the results were to make sense. The problem, for most part, was due to an apparent dissaving phenomenon attributed to the institution of a liberal consumer installment credit about 1964. Dummy variables were appropriately used by Carter and Manhertz and, to a great extent, these help to normalize the situation. While the dissaving tendency remains as shown in footnote 2 and Chapter 5, a dummy variable used for similar reasons was not found to have any explanatory capacity in this study; hence, none was incorporated in its final formulation.[2]

In the present investigation, on the contrary, the consumption function follows conventional lines and is found to relate to current disposable income and the koyck-type distributed lag formulation over previous incomes.

---

[2]See, for example, Manhertz, op. cit., p. 208; Carter, op. cit., p. 184. When personal consumption was made a function of personal disposable income alone, it gives a Coefficient of Determination of 0.96 but an MPC of 1.07. Regressing personal saving with disposable income also gives a negative coefficient, implying a greater increase in consumption for each increment of income received. Moreover, the specification actually used implies that in the long run there will be dissaving as well. More particularly, the ultimate adjustment can be estimated as he present marginal propensity to consume (b) times the reciprocal of 1.0 minus the Coefficient of the previous years consumption. In symbols this is equivalent to:

$$B = b \times \frac{1}{1-dct-1}$$

where B is long run MPC and d represents the fraction of previous years consumption. The last term on the right may

According to this well known permanent income hypothesis, the consumer is assumed to adjust his expenditure according to a weighted sum of his past levels of income, the weights declining geometrically in the form:

$$C_t = k(Yp)_t = k \sum_{i=o}^{\infty} g^i Y_{t-1}$$

which can be reduced to:

$$C_t = kYd_t + gC_{t-1}$$

The form of the function used is:

$$C_t = a + kYd_t + gC_{t-1}$$

In particular, the relation is:

$$C_t = c_o + c_1 Yd + c_2 C_{t-1}$$

---

be seen as a kind of multiplier. In this function B would be:

$$0.7081 \times \frac{1}{1-0.3675} = 0.7081 \times 1.581 = 1.12$$

One interpretation is that B will be 1.12 when consumption is in equilibrium. In general, this can be evaluated as follows:

$$Ct = a + bYd_t + dC_{t-1}$$

where Yd = disposable income.

In equilibrium $C_t = C_{t-1}$

then $C_t = a + bYd_t + dC_t$

$$C(1-d) = a + bYd$$

$$C = \frac{a}{1-d} + \frac{bYd}{1-d}$$

$$\frac{dC}{dYd} = b/1-d = B$$

For a reference to a slightly different interpretation see footnote 3.

40

where the constant term, C_o, suggests that there will be some amount of consumption through depletion of stocks, for example, even if one makes the extreme assumption of no additional income in the economy.[3] The value of the constant term (in Table 3) which indicates that this parameter is significantly different from zero lends additional support to the form which the function takes here.

GOVERNMENT CONSUMPTION

Some aggregate macro-economic models treat the government sector as exogenous to the system.[4] Others exclude it completely and still obtain desirable results.[5]

However, since in the final analysis the overall policies of the economy are greatly influenced and sometimes dictated by the government, explicit inclusion of this sector inevitably sharpens the view on the interrelatedness of all the sectors. Indeed, it is reasonable to assume that in some (developing) economies the major constraint on growth resides in the public policies which originate in the government sector. In fact, the nature of this study and its objectives are, in an indirect way, geared to see

---

[3] One form of the Permanent Income consumption function, it may be observed, does not have a constant term and associates quite frequently with the name of Milton Friedman. For an extended treatment of the Permanent Income Hypothesis see, for example, Michael Evans, Macroeconomic Activity (New York: Harper and Row Publishers, 1969) pp. 19-34.

[4] See, for example, Carter, op. cit.; Dutta and Su, op. cit.

[5] For an example of such an approach see United Nations, Studies in Long Term Projection, op. cit.

the extent to which some of Jamaica's critical public policies affect the health of the economy.

The explanatory variables used for government consumption are the net revenue collected from all sources and the gross domestic product or total economic activity. Like personal consumption, a good fit is obtained as indicated in Table 3. Given the level of output, the elasticity with respect to net revenue is only 0.44, suggesting that there is a greater rate of revenue collection than there is for the rate$_6$ of government expenditure on goods and services.

It is interesting to note, however, that the elasticity of government consumption as it relates to gross domestic product is 1.01, assuming no change in net revenue. This would indicate that current government purchases were keeping pace with the overall economic activity. (The full effect of an increase of income on government consumption would include the indirect effect through revenue. The elasticity presented here is the partial effect, holding revenue constant.)

EXPORTS AS AN EXOGENOUS VARIABLE

Like the government sector, total exports are treated as an exogenous or predetermined variable in many studies.[7] As mentioned in Chapter 1,

---

[6] In this and the following chapters, elasticity is mainly computed at the point of the means. The elasticity for the hypothetical function:

$y = a + bx$ is, accordingly, $E = dY/dx.x/y$

In Chapter 1 where double log functions are principally used, the exponents give the values of the elasticities directly.

[7] In the case of the Carter study, the only small part of exports that is included in a structural relationship is receipts of factor payments. See Carter, Op. cit., pp. 183-4.

42

this is not an unreasonable proposition from the standpoint of most developing countries whose exports usually depend on the wishes and demands of the developed economies. Furthermore, where export items originate in agriculture, the levels of export could depend principally on the weather which is controlled (largely) by nature.[8] The foregoing is quite applicable to Jamaica. The export of bauxite and bauxite products depend, in the main, on demand conditions of the American, Canadian and European markets; and the exports of manufactured goods, primarily to the developed market economies, are sometimes influenced by the gesture to foster trade rather than aid.[9] Similarly, much of the agricultural exports are fixed by quotas or other special condition, especially with England. Accordingly, merchandise exports are assumed to be exogenously determined in this study.

The export of services, on the other hand, are assumed to be determined by the system. More specifically, it is described in equation III.b of Chapter 2 and its evaluation is shown in the first part of this chapter dealing with statistical estimation.

It is, nevertheless, restated below for easy reference:

---

[8]This is sometimes the case with sugar and its.by-products as well as bananas. The problem usually centers around drought, flood rains and hurricane.

[9]The exports of rum and molasses to England and Canada dropped significantly between 1950 and 1968 because of home made substitutes. There is the suspicion that this decline could be greater if there was not the mutual need for a certain amount of trade between Jamaica and these countries. Comments on this issue as well as the figures representing the decline may be obtained from Jeffreyson, op. cit., p. 191.

$$X_s = -85.8180 + 0.3288Y - 0.338 \sum_{i=0}^{n} If_i$$

$$(-2.6729) \quad (4.7432) \quad (-2.7342)$$

The equation suggests that service receipts are positively correlated with output but inversely related to capital accumulation. The inverse part of the relationship is somewhat surprising at first glance. It may be due in part to negative externalities (congestion, pollution, etc.) associated with the capital formation[10] and indus- trialization incident to growth. Since the United States is such a heavy user of tourist facilities in Jamaica, an attempt was made to regress export of services with other local variables along with Economic Conditions, Dispos- able Income and Expenditure on Travel of the United States. Various combinations were tried but the results were not conclusive. However, as was expected, U.S. Expenditure on Travel shows the most consistent positive connection.

---

[10]An interesting specification of receipts from services to foreigners is assumed to be associated with total exports and capital imports and is estimated as:

$$X_s = 200.62 + 0.19X + 0.36Mk$$

$$R^2 = 0.85$$

$$d = 1.13$$

where imports of capital is positively correlated with exports of services in line with expectation. This is understandable because especially during the latter part of the period under review, when most of the bigger projects in the bauxite industry had already been undertaken, increasing amounts of the capital imported find its way into tourism in which most of the earinings from export services are generated. But capital appears to have been widening rather than deepening.

CONSUMER IMPORTS

For convenience, consumer imports are divided into Food and Non-Food categories. They account for 20.9 percent of total imports in 1974, as shown in Table 4. Imports of food alone were 11.7 percent of imports in 1974. It was assumed to relate simply to personal disposable income and, at the margin amounted to about 7.0 percent for the period under review. The elasticity relative to disposable income is 0.963. Although this figure appears high, indicating a general problem with local food production, it is, nevertheless, lower than those obtained from the findings of some other studies of the recent past.[11]

This smaller elasticity obtained here could, however, be an illusion. While a lesser inclination to import food would be symptomatic of greater development in accordance with Engel's law, the situation in Jamaica neither seems to reflect greater significant development nor increase local food production. Rather, it appears to reflect a contrived restriction of food imports to help ease the chronic adverse balance of payments position.

NON-FOOD IMPORTS

As a category, Non-Food consumer imports, including such items as automobiles, household furnishings and other durables, was more difficult "to fit" than would have been previously thought. It seems that the difficulty arose because, unexpectedly, the category which embraces the luxuries -- does not show any significant correlation with variables based on a priori reasoning such as disposable and other types of incomes. Even then, surprisingly, the variable behaves inversely with others like total income, profits, trend and the like.

---

[11]For example, see Harris, op. cit., pp. 154-155.

Ultimately, Non-Food imports was found to be an increasing function of total consumer imports, but a decreasing function of population. The estimates are set out in Table 4. The elasticity on total consumer imports is 1.371 which is not surprising since, on the margin, non-food constitutes as much as 80.9 percent of total imports for consumption compared with 62.2 percent at the beginning of the period.

What is interesting is the fact that as population increases or, in a way, as time passes, non-food consumption tends to decrease. If population were increasing faster than income then this phenomenon would be justified because standard of living would be decreasing. The same would be true if there were evidence of significant expansion of Jamaica's non-food industries. Since neither of these is the case in Jamaica, the answer probably lies in the observation made above that some imports have been restricted in the recent past to alleviate the chronic deficits of the balance of payments.

At this point, it may be timely to observe that, according to the specification of the model, total consumer import (Mc) which consists of food and non-food categories serves as the residual imports. As such, it ensures that imports less exports is the equivalent of external capital inflow. Symbolically, this may be shown as:

$$F = M - X \quad \text{or}$$

$$M = F + X$$

where F is external capital inflow or foreign saving.

In the model:

$$Mc = M - Mk - Mig - Mfs - Mos \quad \text{or}$$

$$M = Mc + Mk + Mig + Mfs + Mos$$

The above equations suggest that, given the

rate of growth of exports, imports can only grow
if a larger amount of capital inflow or foreign
saving enters the country. Alternatively, at a
constant rate of inflow of foreign saving, more
imports are only attainable if exports increase.
Moreover, the general implication is that if there
is a shortage of foreign exchange, it will be felt
most in the exogenous, residual category which is,
in this case, consumer imports. This observation
has important significance for the projections of
Chapter 6 and, accordingly, will be further raised
in that chapter.

CAPITAL GOODS IMPORT

For descriptive purposes only, "capital goods
import" includes both the imports of capital
proper, as well as intermediate goods. For
analytical purposes, however, each is treated
separately, their separate estimates are shown in
Table 4, and each will be discussed in turn
beginning with capital imports. It should be
borne in mind, therefore, that this important
distinction exists and, unless otherwise specified, a reference to capital imports throughout
this manuscript should be taken to mean imports of
capital proper.

CAPITAL IMPORTS

Capital imports are found to be determined by
the amount of fixed investment taking place.
This is not surprising since in general foreign
technology plays a major role in most developing
countries. In particular, in Jamaica capital
imports play a predominant role in the field of
mining (mostly bauxite), refining and tourism.[12]

---

[12]Carter, op. cit., p. 183, shows that on the margin,
approximately 88.0 percent of the investment in mining was
imported from abroad.

The estimates show, in fact, that on the margin more than one half of the capital goods for the country originate abroad. Furthermore, the function suggests that if there is the need for investment expansion, the foreign source must continue to play a correspondingly increasing role, at least in the short run. This is substantiated by an elasticity of 1.073 of capital imports relative to fixed investment.

A similar function in the Harris study gave an elasticity of 1.341 which, when compared with the 1.073 obtained above, suggests that over time the local capital goods industries are being developed. The positive constant term obtained in the estimate of the function for the present study although not significant, also implies that even a weak trend in the local development of the capital industries is expected to continue -- a welcome prospect indeed.[13]

THE IMPORTS OF INTERMEDIATE GOODS

This group accounted for by far the greatest share of imports with 42.0 percent in 1974. It is assumed that the chief determinant of these imports is a group of five sectors: mining, manufacturing, construction, transportation and utilities, because of the high degree of intermediate goods associated with them. With an elasticity of demand of 2.74, it can be seen that the imports need of these items is nothing short of overwhelming.

MISCELLANEOUS IMPORTS

This group of imports concerns itself with service payments to the rest of the world in the form of factor payments and a general category

---

[13]Harris, op. cit., p. 155.

referred to as imports of other services.

FACTOR PAYMENTS

The payment of factors is one of the few variables which showed great instability even with other variables with which it would seem to regress logically. These include various combinations of service exports, capital imports, fixed investment, capital stock and economic activity. In particular, the failure to show some consistent pattern with capital imports or fixed investments constitutes a stubborn mystery. This is so since factor payments connected with these items are usually high in the form of investment income and sometimes even raise some controversy as to what should be the optimum foreign capital injection in a developing economy.[14]

The abortive attempts to get a reasonable regression with the variables mentioned above led to a re-examination of the data and the circumstances surrounding its development. It was discovered that a policy change in the formula for computing the bauxite industry profits and income tax was effected in such a way that they would be expressed in U.S. dollars. The devaluation of the Jamaican currency in November 1967 immediately increased the industry's tax yield to the government by about 16 2/3 percent in terms of Jamaican dollars. Whereas, for example, between 1958 and 1967 the industry contributed approximately 13.0 percent of total tax revenue, in 1968 the share was about 14.0 percent. This meant less profits to the industry and since the latter has the most effect on factor income payments, the impact was reflected from 1968 onwards.[15]

---

[14]See footnote 15 in Chapter 1.

[15]See Jeffreyson, op. cit., pp. 150-169 for an informative review of the history and finances of the bauxite and alumina industry.

One of the consequences of the foregoing
situation was a sharp drop of factor payments in
real terms from $59.6 million in 1967 to $48.3
million in 1968. For compensation purposes, a
dummy variable with a value of 1.0 was used from
1968 to 1974. According to the analysis, an
average of approximately $4.0 million less in
payments resulted. Despite this slowdown, the
elasticity of factor payments on capital imports
remains still high at 1.587.

IMPORTS OF OTHER SERVICES

This group, including such things as non-
merchandise insurance and expenditure on foreign
travel, forms the larger part of service imports
and accounts for 9.0 percent of total payments to
foreigners. Its equation is formulated simply
with gross domestic product and indicates that for
every increment of total output, about 2.8 percent
will be allocated for this purpose. Nor is this
share likely to increase in the forseeable future
since the elasticity compared with the total
output measures only 0.535.

So far, the analysis has dealt with the
overall foreign trade sector and consumption
issues. Government consumption featured importantly in this assessment. The way the government
generates its income from which this consumption
is made is the subject of the next chapter.

CHAPTER 4

G O V E R N M E N T   R E V E N U E   A N D   D E V E L O P M E N T

The goals of fiscal policy include full employment, price stability, economic growth and a healthy balance of payments position.[1] The degree to which these goals are achieved depends, in the first place, on a healthy generation of revenue through government's various revenue-generating instruments. This is formalized for the goal of economic growth by equation (3) in Chapter 2 where it is shown that domestic saving includes government saving which in turn depends on the income that government generates.

Where there is a saving-investment gap, therefore, the problem is sometimes due to the fact that the government fails in its tax effort. When this happens, the debilitating effects on development naturally follow.[2] However, while the absolute revenue yield is important, the relative yield provided through the various instruments is crucial to the development process since they are likely to have different incentive effects, some of which may even be negative. In accordance with the objectives of this book, the government sector is, therefore, highly disaggregated in order to analyze in detail the public financial policies that may be necessary to achieve targeted rates of growth.

---

[1]See, for example, Norman F. Keiser, _Macroeconomics, Fiscal Policy and Economic Growth_ (New York: John Wiley & Sons Ltd., 1964) pp. 13-22.

[2]For a brief summary of the assumptions and problems underlying two-gap models, including the saving-investment gap, see Harris, _op. cit._, pp. 148-150.

STATISTICAL ESTIMATION

As was stated in Chapter 3, the final choice of an equation is reconciled by statistical theory and economic consideration. In the following table is shown the quantitative estimates of the various revenue generating media. As before, analysis will follow.

TABLE 5

Statistical Estimates of Government Revenue[a]

De-pen-dent Vari-able	% Of Net Revenue		Parameters		Inde-pen-dent Vari-able	R^2	d
	1965[c]	1974[b]	Constant	Coeffi-cient			
Tc	33.1	10.7	24.2327 (13.0538)	0.0897 (2.8918)	Y_{5s}	0.452	0.9342
				0.0505 (3.1629)	ETus		
Te	26.9	10.8	−9.86237 (−2.6007)	0.1135 (7.8775)	Y_{5s}	0.816	1.0138
Toi	17.8	20.1	−18.6475 (−2.446)	2.0569 (4.7128)	Y	0.613	1.3910
Tb	26.7	42.6	−9.15675 (−1.7530)	0.5669 (7.7439)	(Pr)	0.811	1.4149
Tpy	19.8	24.1	−47.7457 (−5.0309)	0.1468 (7.2207)	Yp	0.788	0.7627
Tsu	−6.2	−3.1	−5.48677 (−3.2022)	0.0176 (6.4769)	Y	0.750	1.2997
Tgy	1.5	0.2	1.0988 (3.8768)	0.7769 (3.7833)	Trg	0.530	1.5079
				−0.0014 (2.6198)	Y		

[a]Other components of net revenue include Trp, Trg, Trxp and Trxg and may be seen in identity V11.2.

[b]Owing to rounding errors, the percent figures do not add to 100.0 total.

[c]Figures obtained from Harris, op. cit., p. 159.

52

INDIRECT TAXES

Indirect taxes are sometimes defined as taxes which are levied against goods and services. Accordingly, they are[4] assumed to be levied only indirectly on people.[4] For convenience, as well as for greater depth of analysis, this group is further disaggregated into custom duties (Tc), excise taxes (Te) and a general category referred to as "other indirect taxes" (Toi). Together they account for little over 40.0 percent of all revenues. Each subdivision will be examined successively.

CUSTOM TAXES

This is one of the variables which shows great instability in this investigation. Like the few other variables which demonstrate erratic behavior, it does not conform neatly to a priori reasoning nor general economic theory. It is not explained satisfactorily, for example, by other variables such as total or net revenue, imports of goods and services, imports of consumer goods, imports of non-food or total indirect taxes. Moreover, it shows a weak connection with overall economic activity.[5]

---

[4]See, for example, Paul A. Samuelson, Economics (10th Ed., New York: McGraw-Hill, 1976), p. 166.

[5]When, for example, a multiple regression was done with domestic product, indirect taxes and non-food imports, the second largest coefficient of determination (R^2) was obtained; but this was only 0.4235. The complete equation is:

Tc = 11.23 + 0.021Y - 0.126 Tin + 0.150 Mnf
     (2.236) (1.904) (-1.189)   (2.360)
 d =   2.2108

Despite the apparent explanatory power with imports of non-food (Mnf), a simple regression with this variable does not show any appreciable systematic linkage.

This is quite a departure from what was true about ten years ago. A good fit was obtained by simply regressing with consumer imports or total domestic product.[6] However, it is worthwhile noting that while customs duties account for little over 10.0 percent of net revenue today, at that time the fraction was 33.1 percent or nearly one-third of all revenues collected.[7]

The best explanatory variables are shown to be a group of five manufacturing or industrial sectors (Y5s) and expenditure on travel by the United States (ETus). There is a negative relationship with the industrial sector, indicating, perhaps, that as this sector develops and the need for imports falls, so too will the revenue earnings from this source.[8] as is to be expected, therefore, the elasticity on the industrial sector is only 0.936, suggesting what has just been mentioned that the revenues from custom duties will, in general, decline as the industrial sector develops -- or at least so it appears from the present vantage point.

Custom taxes vary, on the other hand, directly with the United States expenditure on travel. This is not quite surprising when it is considered that about four-fifths of all the dollars Jamaica earns from tourism originate in the United States.[9] Furthermore, with an ample

---

[6] For the case of the single regression with consumer imports, see Carter, op. cit., p. 159.

[7] Harris, loc. cit.

[8] As has been indicated before, some doubt is expressed here as to whether the fall in imports is due to a real development in domestic production or the illusion created by a curtailment of imports to buffer a troublesome balance of payments.

[9] See, for example, National Planning Agency, Economic

elasticity of 1.686, using U.S. travel expenses as base, this implies a greater proportionate share of custom duties from this source.

EXCISE TAXES

Excise taxes are found to be explained reasonably well by the group of five industrial sectors referred to above. And its elasticity with respect to this industrial group is 1.515, indicating that it is growing at a much faster rate than these activities taken together.

One of the reasons behind this relatively fast growth -- import substitution in final consumer goods -- is believed to be responsible in part for the decreasing rate of growth registered in the custom duties category. The evidence suggests that some capital and intermediate goods which were spared taxes on entry, increase manufacturing output and hence the corresponding excise taxes.[10]

OTHER INDIRECT TAXES

As Table 5 shows, this group, which generates nearly twice as much as import or excise taxes in 1974, is found to vary positively with the total output of the economy. However, with a negative constant term this implies that the marginal is greater than the average rate of taxation. In

---

and Social Survey of Jamaica-1973 (Kingston: Jamaica Government, 1973), pp. 70-76.

[10]This is consistent with the demonstrated negative correlation of the group of five industrial sectors (Y5s) and customs duties. For similar observations on this situation, see Jeffreyson, op. cit., p. 234; Carter, op. cit., p. 191; Central Planning Unit, Economic Survey Jamaica - 1970 (Kingston: Jamaica Government, 1970), p. 147.

the long run, therefore, this category will assume a greater share of total domestic product.

Using the same relationship, Carter's study of 1965 gave an elasticity of 1.48; but at that time this group formed under 18.0 percent of net revenue.[11] Table 5 indicates that after about ten years, i.e., in 1974, it formed little over 20.0 percent of net revenues collected. And as was mentioned above, this category's faster rate of growth relative to income is expected to continue. Moreover, an estimated elasticity of 2.054 unquestionably underscores this projection.

INCOME FROM GOVERNMENT ENTERPRISES

This variable has not been well behaved traditionally.[12] In part, the reason is due to its comparatively small size. In 1974, for example, it approximated only 0.2 percent of net revenue as shown in Table 5; and on the margin, it often measures just between 0.2 and 0.3 percent of gross domestic product.[13]

After various attempts with several other variables, government enterprise income shows the strongest association jointly with transfers to government and gross domestic product. With respect to government transfers, there is a positive

---

[11]The figure for elasticity is found in Carter, loc. cit.; Harris, op. cit., p.159.

[12]Carter alluded to the difficulty of getting a good fit for this variable in his analysis. See his Model op. cit., p. 187. In the Harris Model, he did not register any coefficient of Determination or Durbin-Watson statistic for this variable, apparently, as a consequence of the weak association it exhibits with the other variables. See his analysis, loc. cit.

[13]Carter, loc. cit.; Harris, loc. cit.

correlation, indicating that revenue from this source will increase as transfers to government increase. However, the elasticity is 0.771 which indicates that, in time, the income from government enterprises will not keep pace with the public sector's intake from transfers.

As regards gross domestic product, there is an inverse relationship. As was to be expected, its elasticity based on total domestic output is less than unity (0.968) which suggests that government's income from its participation in enterprise is likely to decrease as income increases. This finding would be a reversal of what was true a little over a decade ago when the clear indication was that government, as entrepreneur, would expand its income generating propensities.[14]

DIRECT TAXES

As indicated earlier, in general, direct taxes are levied on persons as opposed to goods and services. The principal instruments that will be examined in this study are business profit tax and the personal income tax.[15] As a group, direct taxes was responsible for 66.7 percent or exactly two-thirds of all net revenues collected in 1974. This is a dramatic change in its proportion since 1965, when it accounted for 46.5 percent.[16]

---

[14]Carter, loc. cit.

[15]Business profit tax here is used interchangeable with corporate profit tax. However, the personal basis of the concept of the direct tax would not be altered since for all general purposes the corporation is regarded as a person.

[16]Harris, op. cit., p. 159.

BUSINESS TAXES

While both the personsal and business taxes grew over the last decade, it was the business tax which showed the most rapid growth, moving from 26.0 percent in 1965 to 42.6 percent in 1974.[17] For a long time, however, it was known that this sector had the latent propensity to do much better regarding revenue yield. More specifically, it was observed, for example, that while the corporate tax rate between 1959 and 1968 was some 40.0 percent, the amount of profits actually collected was only 23.0 percent. This problem was largely one of indiscriminate use of tax holidays or direct tax evasion because of inefficient tax evaluation and tax collection mechanisms.[18]

In particular, taxes derived from the bauxite-alumina industry were relatively low over the period under review, although there was the potential for more equitable yield. A modest effort in the form of reorganization of the Income Tax Department in conjunction with tax reforms, for example, yielded an increase of nearly 50.0 percent in 1970.[19] In more recent time, the concerted effort to apply equitable standards to the industry results in increased revenue to the government of over 700.0 percent.[20]

---

[17]Harris, loc. cit.

[18]See, for example, Jeffreyson, op. cit., pp. 227-228; Carter, op. cit., p. 188; Central Planning Unit, Economic Survey Jamaica-1969 (Kingston: Jamaica Government, 1969), pp. 123-127 where the so-called "Reform Budget" increased corporate tax yield by 51.4 percent.

[19]See Central Planning Unit, Economic Survey Jamaica-1970, p. 146.

[20]A completely new approach was taken towards the assessment of taxes from the bauxite-alumina industry in 1974. Formerly, revenues in the form of royalties and taxes were calculated essentially at a relatively small flat rate

Business taxes as a whole is found to be a function of total profits. The elasticity is 1.322, an indication that the relative share of profits allocated for taxes has not only increased during the period under review but this likelihood remains at least in the short run.

PERSONAL INCOME TAXES

Personal income taxes receipts are explained by personal income. The elasticity measures 3.379. This large elasticity suggests the extraordinary means which have been taken to spur personal income tax growth. One such means is the "pay as you earn" (PAYE) system which was introduced in 1953 and which continues to have its impact in subsequent years.[21]

Another reason which accounts for the relatively fast growth of this tax relative to personal income is its progressivity. A progressive tax is one in which a greater proportion of each additional dollar of income is allocated to taxes. Thus, high-income persons pay proportionately more tax. Accordingly, as personal income increases, assuming no increase in evasion or avoidance, there will be disproportionately higher

---

per ton of bauxite. Since 1974, the emphasis in assessing tax revenues has been shifted to a percentage based on the realized price of aluminum ingot on the free market. For a comprehensive outline of this new approach, see Consulate-General of Jamaica, New Regulation for Bauxite Industry; Statement by the Prime Minister: On the Current Bauxite Negotiations; and Jamaica and Bauxite: the case for more revenue, May 1974.

[21] See, for example, Jeffreyson, op. cit., p.234 for the comparative share of Income Taxes for the fiscal years 1951-52 and 1967-68.

increases in taxes generated. This is particularly true in an inflationary environment. Indeed, this same argument was used when personal income tax receipts increased by 44.0 percent between the fiscal years 1972-73 and 1973-74, owing mainly to increases in personal payment to public employees.[22]

One of the problems associated with high income taxes, especially if it is progressive, is the fact that it tends to inhibit individual effort and, ultimately, overall income.[23] In the extreme case, it is reasonable to assume that a 100.0 percent tax on marginal incomes above a certain level would not induce any work since the substitution effect for leisure will understandably outweigh the income effect of work. However, these rates have never been attempted in Jamaica.

In the meantime, care should also be taken in the transfer of the community's potential saving from the private to the public sector since a

---

[22]National Planning Agency, Economic and Social Survey of Jamaica-1973, p.25.

[23]Aside from the fact that income taxes are comparatively easy to collect, it is some of these considerations why many economists favor the sales and expenditure tax rather than taxes earned from income. Moreover, sales and expenditure taxes tend to restrict consumption in preference to saving and this tendency is especially encouraged in developing economies where the constraint to growth quite often resides in insufficient saving. See, for example, Peter T. Bauer and Basil S. Yamey, The Economics of Under-developed Countries (Chicago: University of Chicago Press, 1962), p. 200; Charles P. Kindleberger, Economic Development (New York; McGraw-Hill; 1965), pp. 240-243; Norman F. Keiser, Macroeconomics, Fiscal Policy and Economic Growth (New York: John Wiley and Sons Lit., 1964), pp. 144-147. Here, Keiser discusses induced taxes generated by increased income and an eventual reduction of income owing to a smaller multiplier effect.

reduction in private saving is also likely to restrict local private entrepreneurship with the probable reduction of productivity and income as well.[24] This fear, of course, is not so well founded if the object of the public sector is to help ensure saving and make it available to the public and private sectors for further development purposes.

LOCAL TRANSFERS

Transfers in Jamaica consists of a two way flow of funds from the government to persons (Trp) and from the private sector to government (Trg). These transfers are assumed exogenous to the system in the model, in part, because of their small size. This is particularly true of local transfers to the government which was only 1.20 percent of net revenues collected in 1965.[25] In 1974, it was ony about 0.36 percent.[26] Transfer from government is of a greater magnitude but even so it was a mere 1.69 and 2.16 percent of total domestic product, respectively, for the years 1969 and 1974.[27] The other consideration which accounts for the exogeneity of transfers in this study is the fact that, characteristically, a large part is in effect a gift to its recipients. Accordingly, they often depend on philosophical

---

[24]This possible problem is alluded to in a discussion of "Accelerated Capital Formation:" by Bauer and Yamey, op. cit., pp. 190 - 204.

[25]Harris, op. cit., p. 159

[26]Department of Statistics, National Income and Product, 1974 (Kingston: Jamaica Government, 1974), p. 18. All current values are translated to real terms by the use of a consumer price deflator. Using 1960 as base year, the deflator for 1974 is 268.0 according to this calculation.

[27]Loc. cit. See also Department of Statistics,National Income and Product, 1968, p. 44.

and moral rather than on economic bases. Transfer to government may, therefore, increase or decrease depending on the political party in power. Similarly, transfer from government to people may depend on the current government's philosophy with respect to poverty. Indeed, the intermittent hurricanes which strike Jamaica, leaving some people destitute, raise subjective, value judgement questions as to how conditions should be remedied. Nor can these hurricanes - - natural disasters - - be predicted (long) in advance.

One of the unfortunate ironies associated with local government transfers to persons is the fact that while for most part the aim of these transfers is to effect a more equitable distribution of income, the recipients have a very high marginal propensity to consume. As such, except perhaps for the amounts paid for interest on public debt these payments can be seen largely as an allocation for consumption purposes. Accordingly, since the emphasis should be on saving and investment, care must be taken that funds so allocated are objectively rationalized with these considerations in mind.[28]

FOREIGN TRANSFERS

Like local transfers, foreign transfers are also a fixed proportion of GNP in this model for essentially the same arguments that have already been raised, namely their relatively small size

---

[28] It is my belief that the impact of transfer on national income in a developing economy is more debilitating than in a developed economy. This may be shown from the following national income identities:

$$(1) \quad Y = C + 1 + G$$

Disposable income may be set out as

$$(2) \quad Yd = Y - T + Tr$$

and the unpredictable values they are likely to assume.

As regards size, they approximate 1.20 and 1.30 percent of Gross National Product, respectively, for official transfers from the rest of the world (Trxg) and official foreign payments (Trmg) in 1974. Not only are the fractional amounts of these payments smaller when compared with total domestic product, but even with GNP as base they are often smaller for some years.[29]

Where T is taxes and Tr refers to transfers. Also

$$(3) \quad Yd = C + S$$

Where S is saving. From (2) and (3)

$$(4) \quad Y - T + Tr = C + S$$

Rearranging

$$(5) \quad Y = C + S + T - Tr$$

From (1) and (5)

$$(6) \quad I + G = S + T - Tr$$

Which gives

$$(7) \quad I = S + T - G - Tr$$

Equation (7) indicates that the higher the transfers the less the investment and, therefore, the inevitable stricture on growth - - also suggested, incidentally, by equation (5).

[29]Jamaica, like many other developing countries, currently has a larger gross domestic product than gross national product since the net foreign earnings from factor income is a minus quantity, owing primarily to the comparatively higher earnings of foreign capital. For the percentages quoted, see Department of Statistics, National Income and Product, 1974, pp. 16 and 19.

Naturally, this is one of the major considerations why transfers are not explicitly mentioned in some aggregative models.[30]

In connection with the unpredictability of these variables, it is well known that foreign transfers to the government have been increased if there is a natural disaster. This was true, for example, when the country experienced the Gilda flood rains in 1973.[31] It is also reasonable to believe, and in recent times, it is becoming more and more clear, that Jamaica's stated political philosophy will have significant effects on the gifts and aid it receives from external sources.

External payments by government consist largely of contributions to such institutions as The University of the West Indies, The University Hospital, the Caribbean Development and Inter-American Development Banks. It was observed under local government transfers that any arbitrary gifts to persons who have a high marginal propensity to consume is not desirable - certainly from a purely economic standpoint.

The problem with the foreign transfers to institutions like those mentioned above could be of a different nature. Here, even if these payments are regarded as investments, can the country retrieve all the benefits commensurate with its expenditure? Because of the external economies involved, the country may not be able to optimize its benefits from grants to the University of the West Indies, for example, since Jamaica is, perhaps

---

[30]See, for example, Dutta and Su, op. cit.; Lawrence R. Klein and Stefan Scheicher, "A Macro-Economic Model for Mexico" in Techniques of Model Building for Developing Economies, Research Memorandum No. 91, (Vienna: Institute for Advance Studies, 1975), pp. 56-90.

[31]Jamaica Government, Economic and Social Survey 1973, p. 3

the largest overall proportionate contributor.[32]
Again, from a purely economic viewpoint, care
should be exercised when government transfer
payments are contemplated. And while a larger
economic structure like a federation of the West
Indian States would internalize these special
costs and benefits for the area as a whole,[33] it
is still questionable whether a union, per se,
would solve all the other attendant problems.[34]

SUBSIDIES

In the discussion of both local and foreign
transfers, care was taken to draw attention to the
fact that any arbitrary payment to the private
sector could be undesirable. The argument empha-
sized and focused on irrational payments made to
persons with a high marginal propensity to consume
thereby lessening the overall saving of the community. Subsidies present a similar kind of
danger, for example, where payments are made by
government to farmers who misappropriate the payments -- or the major part -- for consumption
purposes.

---

[32]For a fairly comprehensive treatment of the external economies and diseconomies of production and consumption see William J. Baumol, Economic Theory and Operations
Analysis (2nd Ed.; Englewood Cliffs, New Jersey: Prentice-
Hall, 1965) pp. 368-371

[33]Ibid. p. 371. In particular, a good argument is
raised on the merits of coordinated, instead of independent,
decision making since the former may lead to a more optimal
output.

[34]For an idea of some of these possible problems
see, for example, Jeffreyson op cit., p. 213. See also
H. Brewster, and C. Y. Thomas, The Dynamics of West Indian
Economic Integration. Kingston: Institute of Social and
Economic Research U.W.I., 1967.

This is likely to be the case where payments are made before actual production. Indeed, there was always a real danger when discretionary government expenditure associates with unproductive activities or where it is shifted from the intended beneficiaries.[35]

In conjunction with the foregoing, in Jamaica, one important kind of subsidies which is hard to quantify is that given under the Industrial Incentive Laws. These incentives include concessions through tax holidays, accelerated depreciation, duty free capital and raw materials as well as freedom from tonnage taxes. It is doubtful, however whether the economic benefits accruing to the country are commensurate with the revenues foregone. The tax holiday, for example, is criticised on the grounds that it cannot discriminate according to the profitability of an industry. Accordingly, if an industry makes no profit in the early years, it is argued, the exemption of the tax was not an incentive; and if it makes high profits the tax exemption was not necessary and only reduces government revenue.[36]

It has also been observed that many of the firms operating under these Incentive Laws are organized on a short-run basis only to take advantage of the concessions while they last; that many do not interrelate very well with and, therefore, do not strengthen the rest of the economy; that they are usually capital intensive and do not, in general, ease the unemployment problem; and that to the extent that most of the firms' activities

---

[35]The extreme case would be where the government pays merely to dig and refill holes. Some of the normal problems are cited by Keiser, op. cit., pp. 252-254 and pp. 343-344. For cases where well meaning government grants are eventually "shifted" to the wrong recipients see, for example, Bauer and Yamey, op. cit., pp. 166-171.

[36]Jeffreyson, op. cit., pp. 129-132.

take place in Metropolitan Kingston, they have a minimal impact in agriculture and in the rural areas generally. In short, up to recently, the findings tend to suggest that the revenues given up compared with the benefits appropriated is not justified.[37]

As table 5 indicates, subsidies in quantitative form is found to vary positively with total domestic product. The elasticity is 1.99, indicating that it is likely that a greater share of total output will be allocated to subsidy payments even as a short-run proposition. The observation made above could, therefore, prove useful as a modifying force in considering future subsidy allocations.

---

[37]Ibid., pp. 141-147.

CHAPTER 5

SAVING, INVESTMENT AND PRODUCTION

The aim of this book is to explore the growth prospects of developing economies in general and the Jamaican economy in particular. These prospects depend in the main, upon the resources which can be marshaled for capital accumulation, and the productivity of the investment uses to which they are put. In Chapters 3 and 4 we have examined the expenditure and income behavior of the private (household) and public sectors. Implicit in this analysis, of course, is the evaluation of household and government saving.

In this chapter, we will review our results concerning household and public sector saving, and then extend them to the corporate and foreign sectors. We will then turn to an analysis of investment behavior in Jamaica. With this chapter, we will put into place the final blocks of our model, preparing the scene for the projections and policy analysis to follow.

STATISTICAL ESTIMATION

Like the previous chapters, this section brings together the statistical results of the relevant functions. It is re-emphasized that the final determination of each individual equation is conditioned by the joint consideration of economic and statistical theories, given the prevailing Jamaican conditions.

Table 6 shows the estimated and implied residual coefficients of the saving functions and the other pertinent statistics. As the term

Table 6

Quantitative Estimates of Saving

Dependent Variable	% of Saving, 1974	Parameters		Independent Variable	R^2	d
		Constant	Coefficient			
Sp	-12.9	-	-0.120^{ab}	Yd, Ct-1	-	-
Sg	36.7	-	0.663^a	Rn, Y	-	-
Sb	27.1	5.3877 (1.0925)	0.4251 (6.1501)	Pr (𝒥)	0.730	1.3817
Sd	27.6	29.0066	0.0147	$\sum_{1=o}^{n}$ =Ifi	0.918	1.4248
Smnb	21.6	-	-	-	-	-
Pr (𝒥)	-	71.9699 (-4.8186)	0.2776 (9.4173)	Yn	0.864	1.6660

[a]Implied Residual calculated from the relevant estimates of chapter 2.

[b]This estimate does not consider transfers to government and to the rest of the world and should, therefore, be a bit bigger than the actual figure.

Table 7

Statistical Indices of Investment and Production

Dependent Variable	Parameters		Independent Variable	R^2	d
	Constant	Coefficient			
Y	458.989 (37.2993)	0.1773 (15.7332)	$\sum_{i=o}^{n-1}$ Ifi	0.947	0.8071
Y5s	-39.2400 (-2.2064)	0.4776 (16.9540)	Y	0:954	1.0363
1fg	3.2268 (1.1249)	0.1820 (6.3318)	Rn	0.741	0.5439

suggests, the residual value of personal and government saving are implicitly derived from the marginal value of personal and government consumption calculated in Chapter 3. These residuals need some special comments and a further discussion of them will be undertaken at the appropriate place in the following sections of this chapter. Table 6 also gives an indication of the 1974 percent share of each of the five principal categories of saving used in this study, as well as a function for profits.

Table 7 sets out those stochastic equations having to do with investment and production. The equations are self-explanatory and straight-forward and, accordingly, any elaboration on them will be postponed until later in the chapter where these topics are subsequently discussed.

PERSONAL SAVING

Personal saving is defined as the remainder of personal disposable income after consumption. Based on this definition, if the fraction of personal disposable income going to consumption is ascertained the complementary fraction must necessarily be personal saving. This method is used to estimate the personal saving of the Jamaican economy. If follows, at once, that the first important step is a good assessment of the consumption function.

The problems associated with the estimation of the Jamaican consumption function in recent times have already been discussed in chapter 3 where this function is estimated. One of the problems, it may be recalled, is the fact that the marginal propensity to consume is inclined to be greater than 1.00, suggesting dissaving or negative saving. On reexamination of the data, the latter years of this study do reflect this fact. As was indicated in that chapter, a regression of consumption on disposable income alone gives a negative marginal saving rate of -0.07.[1] Moreover, a trial of saving as a function of disposable income gives a negative marginal saving rate as well but in the order of -0.21.[2]

In view of the foregoing, and based on the theory used in formulating the consumption function of this study, the long-run residual saving rate is estimated to be -0.12 as shown in table 6. This saving rate is, of course, based on the Permanent Income Hypothesis which, in essence, maintains that personal consumption depends on how the consumer perceives the expected level of his income over a long-run time horizon. As such, the saving rate (-0.12) indicated above assumes a long-run rate where consumption is in equilibrium.[3]

---

[1]The actual statistical estimates of this regression is:

$$C = -47.1840 + 1.0721Yd \qquad R^2 = 0.9558$$
$$(-1.7180) \quad (17.3937) \qquad d = 1.9433$$

[2]In this function the quantitative evaluation is as follows:

$$Sp = 104.684 - 0.2180Yd \qquad R^2 = 0.4906$$
$$= \qquad (3.9403) \quad (-3.6721) \qquad d = 1.2204$$

The R^2 of this function, however, implies that there are other determinants of personal saving.

[3]For a derivation of this estimate see footnote 2 in chapter 3. It should be noted that while this method of calculation assumes an eventual steady state, a method which characterizes continuous growth must make further assumptions regarding the annual rate of consumption, thereby introducing other possible errors. Thus the net benefits appear to be trivial at this time and do not warrant the extra energies involved .

For any given year, however, the residual for personal saving may be calculated from the identity of chapter 2 in which it is given by the definition

$$Sp = Yd - C$$

where C is consumption and includes personal transfers to government and transfers by persons to the rest of the world. The value of consumption proper as derived from chapter 3 is

$$C = -39.3281 + 0.7081 \, Yd + 0.3675 Ct-1$$

In line with the permanent income hypothesis referred to above, it is conceivable that consumers in Jamaica spend more than they earn because of high expected long-term income from bauxite, alumina and tourism.[4] It is also conceivable that this negative saving is due, in part, to the demonstration effect of consumption of luxuries in America and Canada.[5] Such consumption is facilitated by consumer credit arrangements.In any case,since personal saving will have an important effect on the rate of development,this is one of the areas where remedial action should be attempted.

---

[4]In fact a trial regression of consumption of disposable income (Yd),and earnings from bauxite and alumina (Eba) gives a good fit and suggests that there might well be this connection between the propensity to consume in Jamaica and expected revenue from the bauxite industry. The actual values of the regression are:

$$C = -81554 + 920Yd +).332Eba$$
$$(-0.2972) \ (11.0666) \ (2.3821)$$
$$R^2 = 0.969 \qquad d = 2.3215$$

[5]Some authors refer to this phenomenon as an external diseconomy of consumption. See, for example, Baumol,op.cit, pp.369 - 371.

GOVERNMENT SAVING

According to the 1974 figures of table 6, government saving forms the largest share of total saving with 36.7 percent. Like personal saving, it is arrived at residually, i.e., the remains of government net revenue after current government expendiure. Based on the theory of this study, government consumption is assumed to be a function of net revenue and gross domestic product. As seen in table 3, both these independent variables are significant and the relation attains a good fit.

In view of these assumptions, government saving is estimated <u>marginally</u> to be 0.663 of net revenues collected, as shown in table 6. At first glance this saving rate of government seems high and, certainly, a simple subtraction of current government expenditure (as it is presently constituted) from net revenues alone, would show a much smaller saving rate. However, since the explanatory capacity of government consumption is assumed to rest both on net revenue and total economic activity, this rate of government saving further assumes a given domestic output.

The estimate of the relevant consumption function for government is restated below:

$$G = -32.436 + 0.3368Rn + 0.1171Y$$

The function states that, given the level of domesic product, for every extra dollar of revenue received by government, 34.0 percent will be used for current expenditure and 66.0 percent for saving, supposedly for investment purposes.

It may be worthwhile noting that what the actual government figures are with respect to government saving, depends on how current government spending or consumption is defined. This area can be very subjective. Are some of the items falling under the category of government

73

consumption more properly a part of investment - - and, therefore, could be regarded as saving? This would, in an indirect way, help to explain the apparently large fraction of the extra net revenue that would be inclined to be allocated for saving. Indeed, an examination of the government's Functional Distribution of Recurrent Expenditure in recent times reveals some items (in the categories of Community, Social and Economic Services) such as "Roads and Waterways," "Transport, Communication and Storage" and "Housing", for example, which clearly have investment characteristics.[6]

What, therefore, the foregoing tend to suggest is that, implicitly at any rate, a reasonable attempt is being made on the part of government to save. This comes out especially strongly in the high marginal saving rate of 0.663 shown in table 6 for given levels of total output. The actual figure for government saving is derived residually from the identity of chapter 2:

$$Sg = Rn - G$$

where Rn is net revenue and G is derived from the function set out above. Whether this effort approximates some desirable level or whether still other adjustments can be made will be further scrutinized in chapter 6.

BUSINESS SAVING

For purposes of this study, business saving is used interchangeably with undistributed corporate

---

[6]See for example, Jamaica Government, Economic and Social Survey - 1973, p. 22

profits. With 27.1 percent of total saving in
1974, it ranks a close third to saving from
depreciation. The amount of saving from business
is assumed to be an increasing function of gross
profits. In particular, the estimate as represented in table 7 suggests that about 43.0
percent of incremental profits wil be retained for
saving and potential investment.

The analysis, therefore, suggests that some
57.0 percent of the marginal corporate profits
will be allocated for taxes, dividends and to a
lesser degree private and public transfers. Since
these entities constitute a transfer of funds away
from the main investment sector to the public and
private households, an interesting question might
be raised as to which is the most efficient
transformer of resources into ultimate output.[7]
To this there can be no easy answer.

If, for example, dividends were to be paid
mainly to the wealthy whose MPC is low, much of
these dividends would likely end up as saving and
perhaps productive investment. Essentially, the
same argument holds for transfers. Taxes to the
government are important for the institution and
maintenance of infrastructure and public goods.
But traditionally the public sector is not the
most enterprising entrepreneur; nor does the
analysis of "Income from Government Enterprises"
in chapter 3 suggests otherwise.

---

[7]One is reminded that compulsory saving through
taxation does not mean that there is a (simple) addition to
the community's resources and the reduced private saving
could also restrict the supply and effectiveness of
entrepreneurship. In discussing "Accelerated Capital
Development", Bauer and Yamey make some sound observations
in this general area. See their work, op. cit., pp. 190 -
204.

On the other hand, if saving by business is used for luxurious housing, or repatriated to the rest of the world rather than ploughed back locally for business expansion, the problem for development will be left unresolved.[8] Since the principal constraint on growth is assumed to be capital in this study, a clear objective is to introduce those policies which are consistent not only with the greatest supply of investment goods but also with the most efficient user.

The above observation is all the more important because business saving is explained by profits which in turn depend on national income. The estimated parameters for the profit function shown in table 6 is

$$Pr \ (11) = -71.9699 + 0.2776 \ Yn$$

This indicates that 28.0 percent of increments to national income go to profits and the negative constant implies an expected rise in the profit share of income. Thus, with passing time, the possible problems alluded to which may be associated with busness saving, such as repatriation of profits and conspicuous consumption, could be magnified unless the proper vigil is implemented.

DEPRECIATION

Saving from depreciation was estimated by way of a relationship with the capital stock. Actually, since there was no figure or value for the stock of captial a proxy for the latter was

---

[8]On the question of foreign capital, Jeffreyson, op. cit., pp. 247-249 offers some enlightened views on the dilemma of developing countries as to the merits and demerits of expatriated profits.

used through the yearly accumulation of fixed investment. Table 6 carries the formulation and resulting estimates.

According to these estimates about 1.5 percent of the incremental capital stock is expected to be lost to depreciation annually. This compares very similarly to a previous fifteen-year period when Harris obtained 1.4 percent using a similar technique. What seems to have changed since that time is the share of total saving going to depreciation. Whereas, for examle, for the period 1950 - 1965 average depreciation ranked first of the categories of saving with a share of 35.7 percent, in 1974 it took a relatively far second place with only 27.6 percent.[9]

However, it should be pointed out that while there is a decided long term decline in the relative share of depreciation, the figure for 1974 is not quite representative since between 1965 and 1971 depreciation was for the most part also the principal source of saving. During that time it alternated as the premiere provider of saving only with net foreign borrowing.[10]

NET FOREIGN BORROWING

As was mentioned earlier, since external borrowing and lending depend on such things as subjective asessments of entrepreneurial skills and political stability, net foreign borrowing has been treated in this study as a predetermined variable. In four out of the ten years between

---

[9]Harris, op. cit., p. 159

[10]See, for example, Department of Statistics, Jamaica, National Income and Product Account, 1974, op. cit., p. 20

77

1965 and 1974 net borrowing from the rest of the
world was the main source of gross saving,
reaching a peak of 43.2 percent in 1971.[11] On
the other hand, in 1974 (table 6) it ranks as low
as fourth of the five avenues generating saving
with only 21.6 percent.

Net foreign borrowing is most important
because, given a target rate of growth, if there
is a domestic saving-investment gap the target can
only be achieved if the necessary funds to fill
the gap are forthcoming from abroad. Thus, in
the absence of foreign aid, where, for example,
the produced goods and services are only
sufficient to meet the consumption needs of the
community, there must necessarily be zero growth,
leaving the society in the so-called vicious cycle
of poverty. Furthermore, this situation will
worsen, and even become catastrophic if, as is
generally the case in developing economies,
population grows at a rapid rate. Foreign
borrowing is also important from the standpoint of
obtaining foreign exchange, without which many
have argued, with justification, that growth in
many a developing country can be thwarted even in
the face of adequate domestic saving. Those who
espouse "two-gap" models are some of the strongest
proponents of this theory.[12]

PRIVATE INVESTMENT

The potential source of investment have been
analyzed under various avenues of saving. The
challenge now remains of translating this saving
into the most productive form of real capital
necessary to propel growth at the most desirable
rates. It follows that policies should be de-

----

[11]Loc. cit.

[12]See footnote 9, chapter 4

veloped to encourage this kind of inducement, although, as was hinted earlier, the private entrepreneur by himself attempts an optimization of his return for each unit of investment.

What is sometimes necessary, however, is policy guidance to ensure that these personal and microeconomic optima are, as much as possible, consistent with the desirable national objective. This is all the more important when it is considered that the private sector controls the giant share of about 85.0 percent of gross investment.[13]

In view of the nature of the model, as well as the contemplated simulation process, overall private investment is treated as an exogenous variable. This includes change in inventories which is treated exogenously more so because of its comparatively small size and its observed erratic behavior.

GOVERNMENT INVESTMENT

Unlike the exogeneity of private investment, government investment is, on the other hand, put in a functional relationship. This is done not because it is absolutely necessary for the solution of the model but mainly out of curiosity since the study is especially concerned with the public sector. As table 7 indicates, government investment is assumed to vary with its intake of net revenue. More specifically, the estimate

---

[13]Private investment of the sample years 1965, 1969 and 1974 was respectively 85.5, 84.3 and 84.1 percent. See Department of Statistics, Jamaica, National Income and Product Account, 1974, op. cit., pp.13 and 20.

suggests that, marginally, about 18.0 percent of the net revenue will be allocated for fixed investment.

It is worthwhile pointing out that government fixed investment discussed here has no obvious or meaningful connection with the Capital Account associated with the Annual Budgetary Estimates of the fiscal year. In the Capital Account, items such as financial assets and transfers are integral parts and these are clearly irrelevant here. [14]

----

[14]See, for example, Jamaica Government, Social and Economic Survey, 1973, pp.20-28.

CHAPTER 6

PROJECTION   FOR   ALTERNATIVE
   GROWTH   TARGETS

The previous chapters have been concerned with the development, specification and analysis of the model, assumed to be an approximate portrayal of the Jamaican economy. The resulting values of the coefficients will be used to make projections in the future, having as the principal objectives, the investment requirements necessary to facilitate the trend as well as accelerated growth rates. The focus will naturally be on the finance of the public sector in concert with the main interest of the subject under review.

However, before using the model as a projection vehicle it is useful and indeed necessary to see the extent to which the entire system of interdependent variables duplicate the past. Hence the model will first be verified for its overall predictive accuracy. Futhermore, there will be a brief discussion regarding the scope of the model as it applies to basic alternative policy measures that may be taken, consistent with a healthier economy.

VERIFICATION AND ACCURACY OF THE MODEL

The verification and accuracy determination of a one-equation model is a simple matter. However, in an interdependent system where predictions have to be made on the basis of other predicted quanti-

---

[1] The predictive quality in this case is immediately determined by the value of the Standard Error of estimate. The same is true for each equation taken in isolation.

Figure 1. Ex post Forecast of Government Consumption: 1959-74

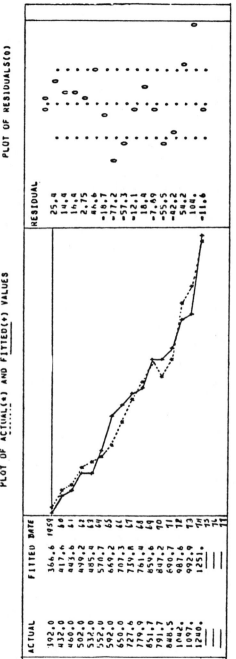

Figure 2. Ex post Forecast of Personal Consumption: 1959-74

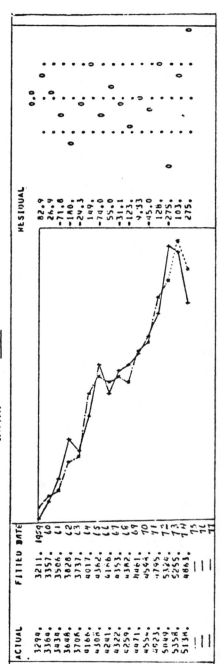

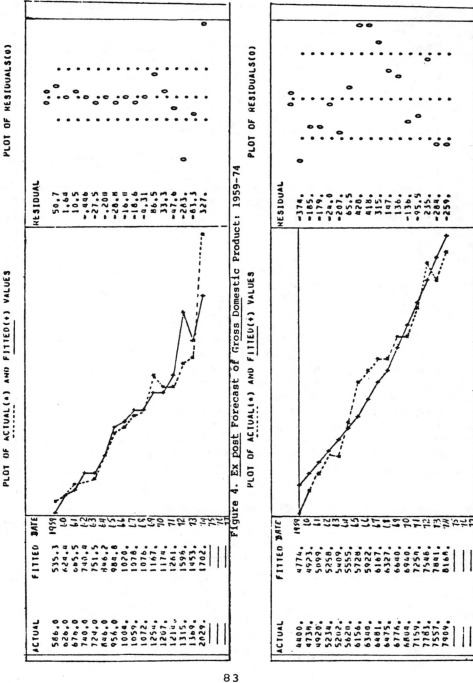

Figure 3. Ex post Forecast of Taxes: 1959-74

PLOT OF ACTUAL(∗) AND FITTED(+) VALUES

Figure 4. Ex post Forecast of Gross Domestic Product: 1959-74

PLOT OF ACTUAL(∗) AND FITTED(+) VALUES

PLOT OF RESIDUALS(0)

PLOT OF RESIDUALS(0)

83

ties, a much more rigorous test is necessary.[2] Accordingly, the total system of equations was used to predict the endogenous variables by use of the exogenous or observed variables for the sample period. Figures 1 to 4, as well as Appendix B, help to indicate this by showing the typical behavior of the model. In general, the simulation process picks up the turning points quite well, and this further helps to attest to the satisfactory specification of the model.

Actually, this exercise provides a test showing the extent to which the model simulates the economic structure from which it was evaluated. In a way, it, therefore, suggests if there is any systematic bias as a result of estimation errors. Nevertheless, this can be considered a limited test since it confines itself to the sample period. Accordingly, the years 1958 and 1975, not included in the sample, were examined as further verification indices. In particular, the values of 1975 will further test the authenticity of the model for extrapolation purposes.

The results of the verification for the main aggregates are shown in Table 8. As indicated in the table, the model behaves generally satisfactorily in its description of the actual path of the economy. During the sample period the correlation between the predicted and the observed values is relatively high. The correlation coefficients are all above 90.0 percent except in the case of fixed government investment where it is approximately 86.0 percent. Furthermore, in five of the nine comparisons made the coefficient, in general, well exceeds the 95.0 percent level. The comparisons of the means as well as the values for the standard deviations and variances also sug-

_____

[2] On the question of methodology of this kind of test see, for example, Harris, op. cit., pp. 164-165. For a more detailed approach see United Nations, Studies in Long Term Projections, op. cit., pp. 64-66.

TABLE 8

COMPARISON OF OBSERVED AND PREDICTED VARIABLES ($m)

Variable	Mean[d]	Standard Deviation	Variance	Correlation Coefficient	1958	1975
Y	6222.0				457.0	835.5[c]
Y[a]	6222.1	247.7	61355.3	0.973	478.0	845.3
M	2817.8				Na	420.1[c]
M[a]	2839.1	192.6	37094.8	0.956	Na	425.4
C	4266.0				33.0	538.6[c]
C[a]	4265.9	130.6	17056.4	0.978	327.0	555.5
G	718.3				42.0	131.3
G[a]	718.2	44.9	2016.0	0.983	40.0	118.7
Y5s	2579.2				167.0	374.5
Y5s[a]	2579.3	112.8	12723.8	0.977	179.0	364.8
Tin	555.2				-	76.5
Tin[a]	555.2	40.3	1619.3	0.934	-	83.5
T	1042.3				33.0[b]	180.3[c]
T[a]	1042.3	114.4	13087.4	0.947	32.0[b]	179.7
Ifg	198.2	-	-	-	Na	Na
Ifg[a]	198.1	40.2	1614.4	0.858	13.0	31.4
Xs	874.6				-	Na
Xs[a]	874.6	59.0	3482.2	0.939	Na	112.5

[a] Predicted figures
[b] Total taxes excluding customs duties
[c] Revised 1975 figures. See Department of Statistics Jamaica, National Income and Product Accounts, 1976
[d] Expressed in $'00,000.

gest no intolerable or systematic bias.

The predicted values derived for the years 1958 and 1975 are also significantly close to the observed values.[3] The average error for the 1975 figures is 3.9 percent; and when personal consumption and government consumption are combined their joint error of 0.6 percent gives an overall error of only 2.4 percent.[4] Hence, it has been concluded that the model behaves sufficiently well to render its use as an extrapolation device for a longer period of time.[5]

---

[3] Despite the fact that the model performs generally satisfactorily as a predictive tool, its efficiency is necessarily dampened not because of the model in itself, but owing to periodic revision in the concepts and definitions in some parts of the data series. Occasionally, this is reflected in quantitative discrepancies not only among some of the respected statistical publications but also between an earlier and later revision of a given publication. See, for example, Jamaica Department of Statistics, National Income and Product Accounts 1974 vs. 1975.

[4] A contributory factor to probable errors in the 1975 figures is due to the fact that in 1974, personal consumption dropped sharply. Accordingly, unlike the other variables which were projected from 1974, 1973 which showed a bigger figure and hence more realistic, was used as a base for the projections for personal consumption. This apparently causes not only a slight overstatement of personal consumption in 1975, but also an understatement of government consumption as well. Interestingly, their joint error, i.e. the error for overall consumption for observed vs. estimated values is only 0.006.

[5] One of the predicted variables which was somewhat off target for 1975 was Indirect Taxes. Many other recognized estimates for this item were overstated for that year owing to what seems to be a short-run phenomenon of a fairly sharp and unexpected decline in the sources comprising this category. See, for example, National Planning Agency, Economic and Social Survey of Jamaica 1975, p. 21.

SCOPE FOR POLICY MEASURES

The verification tests to which the model was subject indicate that it is generally harmonious with the historically observed behavior of the Jamaican economy. This, notwithstanding, the projections based on this history must be made with care especially as the policy parameters were not among the values predicted.[6] As such, it should be re-emphasized that the prospective projections represent linear extensions of the economy's recent historical character, rather than precise predictions of the future.

Conceptually, any of the variables may be projected forward. A solution of the system may involve, for example, finding the values of policy parameters to obtain a given rate of growth. Conversely, the rate of growth may be projected, given the values of policy parameters and exogenous variables. This study focuses on the first approach, one of the objectives being to examine alternative policy measures which may be taken to fill the saving-investment gap if and when such gap is evident.

Within the broad framework suggested above, several options--jointly or individually--lend themselves to policy action.[7] Some of these include: (1) encouragement of long-term capital inflow;[8] (2) aim at increasing the overall domes-

---

[6] Prediction here is taken to mean the values arrived at in the simulated verification process.

[7] A fairly comprehensive set of these possibilities as well as ways in which they may be structurally manipulated is contained in United Nations, Problems of Long Term Economic Projections, op. cit., pp. 9-15.

[8] This alternative has an associating problem which may not be generally important, but should be continuously monitored. See footnote 9, Chapter 2.

tic propensity to save; and (3) aim at increasing the average productivity of capital.[9]

To the extent that a trade gap appears to be a separate problem in our projections, export expansion and import substitution may be seen as additional policy options. Such a problem, in fact, does arise in our projections. The impossibly small size of the residual category "consumption imports" in high-growth projections, suggests that foreign exchange may, indeed, be viewed as a separate constraint even in our one-gap approach.

Obviously, any of the general policy measures, in turn, lends itself to different alternative approaches. The actual method and procedure of implementing a particular line of action, however, fall within the prerogative of the state and as such the final choice of measures taken, largely defies economic analysis. One would hope, nevertheless, that actions taken by government are in keeping with the highest standards of economic rationality.

MAINTAINING HISTORICAL GROWTH TRENDS TO 1985

It has been shown in Chapter 1 that there has been a recent tendency toward retarded growth in the Jamaican economy. One of the first priorities in the development process, therefore, should be an attempt to arrest this trend and ensure that the economy continues to grow at least as well as it has done over the last ten or fifteen years.

---

[9] The classic way of achieving this objective is to shift, where possible, investment to those projects with low capital intensity. In the early stages of development this may not be feasible, however, as large amounts of capital per unit of labor are usually necessary for infrastructure development.

Over the fifteen-year period between 1959 and 1974 the compound growth rate of the economy was 3.9 percent. Using this period as base, it follows that the economy must continue to grow at this rate to 1985 in real terms merely to maintain the present rate of growth of the standard of living, assuming for the moment that the population is also growing at its historical rate. The question now arises as to what the prerequisites must be if this growth rate is to be maintained. The answer, of course, rests with the model.

Under the specifications of the model, total output depends on gross capital formation which reflects the gross periodic or annual investments. The model also indicates the equivalence of saving and investment. The problem is, therefore, reduced to the equivalent values of <u>planned</u> saving and <u>planned</u> investment which must be forthcoming to achieve a continuous rate of growth of 3.9 percent. According to the characteristics of the model, gross domestic product (Y) and gross investment (I) must grow at the same rate.[10] Theoretically, therefore, if <u>ex ante</u> saving and <u>ex ante</u> investment are both increased at a constant rate of 3.9 percent, this should provide sufficient fuel to keep the economy at this steady state of increase into the future.

---

[10] The fact that output and investment will grow at the same rate under these circumstances may not be completely clear. However, one way of verifying this is as follows:

From the model

$$Y = kK \qquad (1)$$
$$dY/dK = k \qquad (2)$$
$$dY = kdK = kI \qquad (3)$$
$$dY/Y = kdK/Y \qquad (4) \quad \text{(dividing both}$$

but from (1) $\quad k = Y/K \qquad\qquad\qquad$ sides by Y)

and $\qquad\quad 1/k = K/Y \text{ (substituting)}$
$$dY/Y = dK/K$$

In the actual solution of the system, once the sixteen predetermined (exogenous and lagged endogenous) variables are given, a unique solution presents itself, consistent with the overall assumptions made. Accordingly, to aid in its solution the following assumptions were made:

The projected values of all transfers were based on their average annual percent of GDP over the five-year period between 1970 and 1974. Thus, internal transfers to government (Trg) and from government (Trp) were projected at 0.14 and 2.30 percent; external receipts by persons (Trxp) and government (Trxg) projected at 2.90 and 1.04 percent; and external payments by persons (Trmp) and government (Trmg) projected at 2.4 and 1.3 percent of GDP. A similar average was calculated for export of factor services (Xfs), inventory investment (In) and net foreign borrowing (Snmb) and these were, therefore, projected at 1.7, 0.94 and 7.8 percent of GDP, respectively.

The assumption relative to population was based on the observed 1.5 percent compound growth rate over the sample period or the last sixteen years before 1975. Similarly the growth of goods exports (Xg) and USA expenditure on travel (Etus) are assumed to continue to grow at their observed compound rates of 5.4 and 4.3 percent, respectively, over the ten years previous to 1975. The dummy [variable (D_1)] which is an independent variable of factor service imports (Mfs) continues with a value of 1.0; and the lagged endogenous variables of consumption (C_{t-1}) and capital (Σ Ifi) are automatically generated as the system is projected forward. The complete solution is given in Appendix A1.

The following table shows how some of the main national income aggregates will be affected over the next decade if the economy grows at historical rates. It also indicates the sources of fiscal policy and suggests the role the latter must play if the <u>scheduled</u> saving and investment are to be achieved.

Table 9

Trend Growth of National Income Aggregates and Government

Sector: 1975-1985

Variables	(1) 1975	(2) 1980	(3) % CH.	(4) 1985	(5) % CH.
Gross Domestic Product (GDP)	845.3	1017.4	20.4	1229.7	45.6
Consumption (C)	555.5	645.1	16.0	757.3	36.2
Gross Investment (I)	198.9	240.4	20.6	290.6	45.7
Fixed Private Invest. (Ifpr)	159.5	191.0	19.4	228.7	76.9
Fixed Gov't Investment (Ifg)	31.4	39.8	29.0	50.2	61.3
Government Purchases (G)	118.7	154.3	29.4	198.4	66.4
Exports (X)	361.5	457.9	26.5	582.8	61.0
Imports (M)	425.4	534.8	25.9	675.8	59.1
Net Gov't Revenue (Rn)	154.9	200.9	30.5	258.0	66.5
Indirect Taxes (Tin)	83.5	102.5	22.6	126.0	50.0
Direct Taxes (TD)	96.2	129.7	35.4	171.4	78.1
Business Taxes (Tb)	55.8	75.1	33.9	99.1	76.8
Personal Income Taxes (Typ)	40.4	54.6	37.5	72.3	80.0
Gross Saving (S)	198.9	240.4	20.6	290.4	45.7
Gov't Saving (Sg)	36.2	46.6	30.6	59.6	66.7
Personal Saving (Sp)	-21.9	-34.3	54.5	-50.6	131.8
Business Saving (Sb)	54.4	69.0	27.8	87.1	61.1
Saving from Depreciation (Sd)	64.2	79.7	25.0	98.4	53.1
Net Foreign Borrowing (Snmb)	65.9	79.4	19.7	95.9	45.5

Col. 3 = Col 2/Col. 1 - 1.00
Col. 5 = Col 4/Col. 1 - 1.00
% Ch. = Percent Change

As was to be expected, Table 9 is quite informative and, in effect, represents what may be seen as a rough, possible ten-year plan for the Jamaican economy, assuming that only the modest historical growth rate of 3.9 percent is contemplated. To accomplish even this growth rate, however, it is evident from the table that planned saving and investment must also increase by 3.9 percent per annum for a total increase of 20.6 percent by 1980 and 45.9 percent by 1985. Alternatively, approximately 23.6 percent of GDP per annum must be set aside for total investment or about 22.5 percent of fixed investment if this target is to be maintained.[11]

It is interesting to note, according to these estimates, that over the ten-year period government investment would have to grow at a higher rate than GDP; while private investment would lag behind for the first five years only to overtake both the GDP and government investment in the second five year period.[12] It is also noteworthy that in order to achieve this moderate growth, personal consumption must be fairly well restricted behind the growth of total output, increasing only about 16.0 percent by 1980. On the other hand, the table suggests that government consumption increases at a much greater rate than the growth of the economy. While a high marginal propensity to consume on the part of government in developing countries is sometimes defended on the

---

[11] It should be noted that, in accordance with the model, the incremental capital-output ratio is associated with fixed rather than total investment. The latter concept includes changes in stock or inventories. It should be noted, too, that where small discrepancies arise, these are attributed to rounding errors and problems of aggregation.

[12] This is not unusual in a developing country where government first invests heavily on infrastructure which in turn induces the business community, both local and foreign, to initiate and expand its own investment projects.

grounds that a developing society needs better education, health care, etc., it is also not unusual that a good deal of waste exists in the process of implementing some of these services.

Of the categories which comprise total saving, personal saving is the most volatile and, as observed in the table, it is expected to show a comparatively high negative balance by 1985. Furthermore, it expresses by far the highest increase of 131.8 percent. Since personal consumption is somewhat curtailed, and private transfers to government are negligible, the problem seems to be due in part to private transfers by Jamaicans to the rest of the world.[13]

For compensation purposes, it is necessary that the other kinds of saving on the average grow much more than total saving as a whole. If net foreign borrowing just about keeps pace with the growth of total saving, government and business saving, both productive sources, can provide the necessary amount to accomplish the stated goal.

What part must taxes and government revenue play over this period of time? As indicated in the table, net revenues of government will grow from \$154.9 million in 1975 to \$258.0 million in 1985, a growth rate which is much faster than the growth of the economy as portrayed by a terminal increase of 66.5 percent compared to 45.6 percent increase for GDP. Of the two major categories of taxes, direct taxes are increasing over one and one-half times the indirect category and are expected to generate some \$171.4 million by 1985. Within the direct taxes group, personal income

---

[13] It is worthwhile recalling that personal saving (Sp) is defined as: $Sp = Yd - C - trg - trmp$ where Yd is disposable income, C is personal consumption and trg and trmp are local transfers to government and private transfers to the rest of the world, respectively. As mentioned elsewhere in this study, the tendency of having dissaving in Jamaica as a whole has been evident for some time.

taxes register the fastest rate of growth and, in fact, except for personal saving, it shows the greatest rate of increase of all the entries listed. It is true that continuous increase in the personal income tax is likely to have a negative feedback effect on the supply of labor but this question is dealt with elsewhere in this study. The foregoing analysis thus indicates that the government sector is likely to have (and perhaps should have) a bigger share of total economic activity even if sheer momentum were to drive the economy along. In 1975, for example, total public demand, including government purchases and fixed capital formation, amounted to $150.1 million or 17.8 percent of GDP. By 1980 this similar share would be 19.1 percent and in 1985, 20.2 percent. On the supply side net revenues generated show a similar pattern, moving from 18.3 percent of GDP in 1975 to 19.8 in 1980 to 21.0 percent in 1985.

INVESTMENT NEEDS FOR ACCELERATED GROWTH

The previous section was concerned with the investment needs to maintain past growth trends. This section answers the question: how must the structure of the economy change to accommodate accelerated rates of growth? Here again, this fundamental question can best be answered through the instrumentality of the model.

Characteristically, the model states that growth is a function of the saving ratio and the incremental capital-output ratio.[14] In particular, it states that growth (g) is directly related to the saving ratio (s) and inversely related to

---

[14] In general where the production function is homogenous such as the basic one that is used in this study, the marginal and average productivity of capital are the same and hence the capital-output ratio and incremental capital-output ratio are also the same. However, the assumption made in this study to evaluate the capital stock, essentially reduces this production function to a non-homogenous one.

the incremental capital-output ratio (k).[15]   In
symbols this may be represented as

$$g = \frac{S/Y}{dK/dY} = \frac{s}{k}$$

This implies, at once, that if growth is to increase either that the saving rate must be increased or the capital-output ratio must be
reduced.   Since the model assumes a constant
capital-output ratio, the candidate which must be
varied is the saving ratio.

   Based on the above expression it is now a relatively simple matter of finding the amount of
saving and, therefore, investment that will be
needed for given rates of growth:

$$s = S/Y = gk$$

$$S = I = gkY$$

With a statistically derived incremental capital-
output ratio of 5.65 this means, for example, that
the saving ratio should be 0.283 if a 5.0 percent
growth is expected.[16]

---

[15] To derive this let:
dy/Y = growth rate; S/Y = Saving ratio; dK/dY = I/dY =
incremental capital-output ratio.   Since $S = I$, $S/Y = I/Y$.
But $dY/Y = \frac{I/Y}{I/dY}$
The above expression thus states that growth is equivalent
to the saving rate divided by the incremental capital-output
ratio.

[16] The estimated capital-output ratio of 3.7 referred
to in Chapter 4 compared with this incremental rate of 5.65
suggests that there is, in fact, capital deepening in the
economy.

In order to accelerate the rate of economic growth, the specification of the model calls for an increase of the saving and, therefore, investment ratio. In general, saving for the community can be increased indirectly by government action such as taxation or even through its stated political philosophy and ideology.[17]

Since the focus of this study is on the government sector, the emphasis will, therefore, be to curtail, within reason, government consumption as well as to increase taxes and see how the economy reacts to these changes. Naturally, it should be borne in mind that the more emphasis is placed on growth the more austere the program of development must be. These considerations aside, the central questions that this section attempts to answer include: (1) what can be done in the very short run to foster a faster rate of growth; (2) what direction the action should take; and (3) what is the magnitude of the problem.

The solution of the model, giving the quantitative estimates of all the variables at different levels of growth above the historical rate may be seen in Appendix A.2 to A.4. Table 10 summarizes some of the macroeconomic aggregates as well as other key variables, the path they are likely to assume, and the magnitudes that they are likely to

---

17 One of the uses of taxation, in general, is the forced saving which is created for the economic community. Futhermore, government induced inflation will increase saving if the tax system is progressive and/or because the rise in prices will transfer income from consumers to investors. Kindleberger, op. cit. pp. 101 and 226-230. It is noteworthy, too, that net foreign borrowing could also be increased or decreased depending on the changes in government's political philosophy and the climate it creates for stability.

TABLE #10

KEY VARIABLES [a] AND ALTERNATIVE GROWTH TARGETS: 1975 - 1980 [b]

GROWTH RATE (%) VARIABLES	1975					1978					1979					1980				
	4.5	4.6	5.4	5.8	6.0	4.5	4.6	5.4	5.8	6.0	4.5	4.6	5.4	5.8	6.0	4.5	4.6	5.4	5.8	6.0
GDP	845	845	845	845	845	961	964	979	988	994	1005	1010	1033	1047	1055	1050	1057	1091	1110	1121
C	545	543	534	497	474	599	598	585	538	508	622	621	611	562	532	645	645	639	584	558
I	232	239	278	297	307	268	277	334	364	382	280	291	353	387	407	293	304	373	410	433
IFP	194	201	241	254	260	223	232	290	313	325	233	243	306	332	346	243	254	323	352	368
IFG	31	30	29	35	39	36	36	35	42	47	38	38	37	45	51	40	40	40	48	54
C	78	70	69	78	84	96	87	87	98	107	103	94	95	107	117	110	100	103	117	
X	361	360	360	360	360	417	417	418	418	418	438	439	440	441	441	461	461	464	465	466
M	424	424	474	474	474	490	490	549	551	552	514	515	579	582	584	540	541	611	615	617
RN	150	149	144	175	199	179	179	175	213	241	191	190	188	229	260	202	203	202	247	280
TIN	84	84	93	130		96	96	97	109	152	100	101	102	115	161	105	105	108	122	171
TD	92	90	85	105	92	113	112	108	132	117	121	121	118	144	129	130	130	128	157	141
TB	53	52	49	55	47	65	65	62	70	61	70	70	68	77	68	75	75	74	84	75
TYP	39	38	36	50	45	48	47	46	62	56	51	51	50	67	61	55	55	54	73	66
S	232	239	378	297	307	268	277	334	364	382	280	291	353	387	407	293	304	373	410	433
SG	72	79	75	98	115	83	92	88	115	134	88	97	93	182	143	92	102	99	130	153
SP	-23	-23	-27	-29	-30	-27	-27	-25	-21	-19	-30	-30	-28	-24	-21	-33	-33	-32	-27	-25
SB	52	52	49	47	42	62	61	59	57	51	65	65	64	61	55	69	69	68	66	60
SD	65	65	65	65	65	75	76	78	79	80	79	80	83	84	85	83	84	88	90	91
SNMB	66	116	116	116		75	75	134	135	136	78	79	142	144	145	82	83	150	152	154

a. The symbols of these variables are the same as those given in parenthesis in table 9 to which reference can be made in case of doubt as to their meaning. This is done to accommodate more years in the table.

b. Figures are in 1960 prices and are rounded to the nearest whole number.

97

attain in the immediate future under varying degrees of development targets. The table itself is self-explanatory. Perhaps, however, the first significant pattern the figures reveal is the generally expected fact that in a developing country the speed of development is inversely related to consumption and directly related to investment.[18]

As regards consumption, this is made especially obvious for personal consumption in a given year. For example, according to the table, in 1978 personal consumption would be approximately $600.00M if only a 4.5 percent growth is expected; but little over $500.00M if the 6.0 percent growth target were to be achieved. The pattern is all the more illuminating since in no case was any one of the coefficients in the model representing the private sector changed or manipulated. Rather, this is accomplished through the sole interdependency of the variables of the system. Similarly, investment in 1978 must increase from $268.00M at a growth rate of 4.5 percent to $382.00M or an additional 42.5 percent to get a 6.0 change in total output.

A reference to Table 9 shows that to satisfy the trend rate of growth of 3.9 percent, gross saving to the tune of $198.9M in 1975 was necessary. According to Table 10, it would be necessary to increase gross saving to $232.00M to speed up the growth rate to 4.5 percent. This could be achieved simply by changing the coefficient of GDP relative to government purchases from 11.7 to 7.1 percent. Thus, the expression of government con-

---

18 Note that in a developed economy a reduction of consumption is likely to retard growth since the increase in saving acts like disinvestment with a negative multiplier effect.

sumption as it relates to the rest of the system is now:

$$G' = -32.436 + 0.337 \text{ Rn} + 0./0714Y$$

as against

$$G = -32.436 + 0.337 \text{ Rn} + 0.1174Y$$

in the orginal expression. Similarly, a further reduction of government purchases from 0.337 to 0.285 of net revenue (Rn) would raise the level of saving to $239.00M in 1975 needed for a 4.6 annual increase of total output.

In view of the fact that there must be practical minimum limits on government purchases, other avenues must now be exploited as sources of saving. The other candidate which readily presents itself as a source of saving and which is influenced directly or indirectly by government policy is net borrowing from the rest of the world. A rate of growth of 5.4 percent from the 4.6 percent just discussed would necessitate a saving gap of $39.00M in 1975, $56.00M in 1978 and $69.00M in 1980. This is attainable if in addition to the overall reduction of government consumption just described, foreign saving (Snmb) increases from the historic trend rate of 7.8 to 13.7 percent of GDP. Further to the measures already taken, much more will have to be done to generate saving if total product is to attain still higher rates of increase. The government can, therefore, change tax rates. For example, for the $297.00M and $410.00M saving and investment necessary in 1975 and 1980 respectively to achieve the 5.8 percent growth mark, the following can be done in addition to measures taken so far:

1. Change incremental personal income taxes (Typ) from 14.7 to 18.0 percent of income (Yp)

2. Change incremental business taxes (Tb) from 56.7 to 66.0 percent of profits ($\hat{\Pi}$)

3. Change incremental excise taxes (Te) from 11.4 to 15.0 percent of manufacturing (Y5S)

99

4. Change incremental custom taxes (Tc) from 9.0 to 10.0 percent of Y5S

5. Change incremental subsidies (Tsu) from 1.8 to 1.5 percent of GDP.

Finally, if the objective were to grow by 6.0 percent per annum there would still be a saving gap of $10.00M to be filled in 1975 and this would be amplified to $23.00M by 1980. This can be done by raising the incremental rate of all other in-direct taxes as a group (Toi) from 5.7 to 10.0 percent of gross domestic product. Of course the other saving generating mechanisms that were pre-viously instituted must be in place to render this possible.

Let us now consider the stress that some of the other key variables must undergo especially at the higher rates of growth in order to make them possible. In 1975, for example, imports at the 4.5 percent growth rate amounted to $425.00M and by 1980 at the 6.0 percent level it must assume a scale of $617.00M, changing the trade gap under the circumstances from $63.00M to $151.00M--quite a high absolute amount by Jamaican standards.

The potential problem relating to the trade gap was already raised in Chapter 3 in the discus-sion of consumer imports (Mc) which is the resi-dual exogenous factor of imports. As was shown in that chapter,

$$F = M - X$$

where F represents capital inflow or foreign sav-ing. And

$$Mc = M - Mk - Mig - Mfs - Mos.$$

By assumption, exports of goods (Xg), the greater part of exports is growing at a constant rate of only 5.4 percent consistent with the historical rate of growth of GDP of 3.9 percent. Thus, as the above equations suggest, at the higher rates of growth which necessitates higher imports

100

(especially of capital and intermediate goods) the increasing trade gap will also mean an increasing shortage of foreign saving or foreign exchange to purchase total imports. Hence, the residual exogenous category, Mc, must necessarily absorb most of the stress.

A manifestation of the above argument is amply reflected in the 6.0 percent level of projected growth (Appendix A.4) where it is shown that from 1977 onwards the sums available to purchase consumer imports (Mc) are so unreasonably small that they assume negative quantities. To a lesser degree, the problem is also exemplified at the 5.4 percent level shown in Appendix A.3.

Imports of non-food (Mnf) which is itself a function of consumer imports (Mc), thus becomes negative as well. Futhermore, imports of non-food is also negatively correlated with population, implying that over time as population increases, non-food imports will decrease. This further suggests that if there is a foreign exchange shortage, the least priority will be given to non-food imports such as cars and washers. Here again, this is borne out in Appendix A.4 where as early as 1975 non-food imports of $0.90 million was the smallest value of any of the categories of imports; and this continues to be the case through 1985 where the figure attains a magnitude of -$165.50 million.

An assessment of the foregoing leads to the conclusion that the model is obviously sending out danger signals. In effect the message relayed is: either foreign saving or exports or both must grow faster than they have been growing so far, or the higher rates of growth cannot be achieved unless there is a corresponding increase in import substitution.

ALTERNATIVE GROWTH TARGETS TO 1985

The last section assesses the size of the problem and describes the structural changes that may

101

TABLE 11

KEY VARIABLES [a] AND ALTERNATIVE GROWTH TARGETS: 1981 - 1985 [b]

GROWTH RATE (%) VARIABLES	1981					1983					1984					1985				
	4.5	4.6	5.4	5.8	6.0	4.5	4.6	5.4	5.8	6.0	4.5	4.6	5.4	5.8	6.0	4.5	4.6	5.4	5.8	6.0
GDP	1098	1107	1152	1177	1192	1201	1214	1284	1323	1346	1255	1271	1355	1402	1430	1313	1330	1431	1487	1520
C	670	670	669	618	586	723	725	734	683	649	751	754	769	718	684	780	875	807	755	721
I	306	319	394	435	460	334	349	439	489	519	349	366	463	518	551	365	383	488	549	586
IFP	253	266	340	373	391	276	291	378	417	440	288	304	398	442	467	300	318	420	468	495
IFG	42	42	43	52	58	47	47	48	59	67	50	50	52	63	71	52	53	55	67	76
G	118	108	110	127	138	134	123	130	149	162	143	131	140	161	176	152	140	150	173	180
X	484	485	489	491	493	535	537	544	547	550	563	565	573	578	581	592	594	604	610	613
M	567	569	644	650	653	626	628	716	725	731	658	661	755	767	773	691	694	797	810	818
RN	215	215	217	265	301	241	242	249	306	348	255	257	266	328	374	270	272	284	351	401
TIN	110	110	113	129	181	120	121	126	144	204	126	127	122	152	216	132	133	140	161	229
TD	140	140	139	171	154	159	160	164	201	184	170	171	177	218	200	180	182	191	235	217
TB	81	81	80	92	82	92	92	94	109	99	98	99	102	119	108	104	105	110	129	118
TYP	59	59	59	79	72	67	68	70	92	85	72	72	75	99	92	76	77	81	106	99
S	306	319	394	435	460	334	349	439	489	519	349	366	463	518	551	365	383	488	549	586
SG	97	108	106	139	163	107	120	119	157	186	112	126	126	167	198	118	133	134	178	211
SP	-37	-37	-36	-32	-29	-44	-45	-45	-41	-38	-49	-49	-50	-46	-43	-53	-53	-55	-51	-49
SB	73	73	73	71	65	82	82	84	82	76	86	87	89	88	82	91	92	95	95	88
SD	87	88	93	96	97	97	98	105	109	111	101	103	111	116	119	106	108	118	124	127
SNMB	86	86	158	161	163	94	95	176	181	184	98	99	186	192	196	102	104	196	204	208

a. The symbols of these variables are the same as those given in parenthesis in table 9 to which reference can be made.

b. Figures are in 1960 prices and are rounded to the nearest whole number.

be made to steer the economy on a path which is consistent with increasing levels of growth. But the figures only reflect the size of the problem in the shortrun. This section seeks to evaluate the growing need of the economy at these same rates of growth as an intermediate or long-run proposition, given the changes that have been recommended. This section will, therefore, give a better appreciation of the gigantic task which lies farther ahead in finding the resources necessary for the more ambitious growth targets. Furthermore, it will give a better understanding as to the degree of tentative structural change the economy will undergo when some of the recommended changes have had more time to have their full impact.

Table 11 sets out the more pertinent variables and the values they will assume by the year 1985. Like Table 10, too, one is readily reminded, according to the relative values of the appropriate figures, that to obtain increasing levels of growth, consumption must be reduced and saving as well as investment correspondingly increased, ceteris paribus.

When one compares Table 9 which shows the trend figures with this table, the comparison reveals that if the least ambitions target of 4.5 percent were instituted the GDP in 1985 would be increased by about 55.0 percent; while if the most ambitions target of 6.0 percent could be implemented the resulting GDP with a value of $1,520.00M would nearly double itself. However, to sustain this 6.0 percent target, saving and investment would have to be about $586.00M in 1985 or roughly a tripling of the resources that are presently earmarked for growth purposes.[19]

---

[19] The explanation for the faster rate of growth of investment is due to the fact that at the higher rates of growth investment must increase if the capital-output ratio is assumed to be constant.

This does not mean, of course, that the standard of living would not increase over the time when these sacrifices are made. In fact at the 6.0 percent level of growth the standard of living would be about 30.0 percent higher in 1985 compared with 1975, assuming that population maintain its rate of growth.[20] This fact is also reflected in Table 12.

In terms of sheer size, many of the growth-promoting variables, according to the table, must be approximately doubled and in some cases more than doubled over the short period of four years between 1981 and 1985 if the 6.0 percent target is to be attempted. These include net government revenue, indirect business taxes, government saving and net foreign borrowing. Table 12 gives a comparison of the estimated structure of the economy in 1975 with what it should be in 1985 under the prevailing assumptions at the different rates of growth. While this table gives another perspective to the analysis it is interesting to note that it essentially substantiates the arguments that have already been raised.

First, it indicates that in 1975 the estimated share of personal consumption was 65.8 percent but this would be reduced to 61.5 percent in 1985 if the trend rate (3.9) percent is assumed and as low as 47.4 percent if the target is 6.0 percent.

Second, the saving and investment rate accounts for only 23.6 percent of GDP at the trend rate but must increase to as high as 38.6 percent of total output at the 6.0 percent level. During the process the indication is that a comparatively greater share of the investment will be done by business, moving from 18.6 to 32.6 percent of GDP

---

20 All the figures and comparisons are discussed in real terms so the question of inflation would not alter the conclusions drawn.

TABLE 12

STRUCTURAL COMPARISON OF THE ECONOMY: 1975 AND 1985 [a]

VARIABLES	1975 TEND[b]	1975 %GDP	1985 TEND[b]	1985 %GDP	4.5%	%GDP	5.4%	%GDP	6.0%	%GDP
GDP	845	100.0	1230	100.0	1313	100.0	1431	100.0	1520	100.0
C	556	65.8	757	61.5	780	59.0	809	56.0	721	47.4
I	199	23.6	290	23.6	365	27.8	488	34.1	586	38.6
IFPR	160	18.9	229	18.6	300	22.8	420	29.4	495	32.6
IFG	31	3.7	50	4.1	52	4.0	55	3.8	76	5.0
C	119	14.1	198	16.1	152	11.6	150	10.5	180	11.8
X	362	42.8	583	47.4	592	45.1	604	42.2	613	40.3
M	425	50.3	676	55.0	691	52.6	797	55.7	810	53.8
RN	155	18.3	258	21.0	270	20.6	284	19.8	401	26.4
TIN	84	9.9	126	10.2	132	10.1	140	9.8	229	15.1
TD	96	11.4	171	13.9	180	13.7	191	13.3	217	14.3
TB	56	6.6	99	8.0	104	7.9	110	7.7	118	7.8
TYP	40	4.7	72	5.9	76	5.8	81	5.7	99	6.5
S	199	23.6	290	23.6	365	27.8	488	34.1	586	38.6
SG	36	4.3	60	4.9	118	9.0	134	9.4	211	13.9
SP	-22	-2.6	-51	-4.1	-53	-4.0	-55	-3.8	-49	-3.2
SB	54	6.4	87	7.1	91	6.9	95	6.6	88	5.8
SD	64	7.6	98	8.0	106	8.1	118	8.2	127	8.4
SNTB	66	7.8	96	7.8	102	7.8	196	13.7	208	13.7

a. The value of the variables are rounded to the nearest whole number.

b. The trend rate of growth is estimated at 3.9 percent compounded.

between the lowest and highest rates of growth. In the meantime, the public sector further demonstrates, as was suggested earlier, its supremacy as the most efficient supplier of saving as its share of GDP increases from a low 4.3 percent in 1975 to a high of 13.9 percent in 1985.

This, of course, is possible because, simultaneously, net government revenue and particularly indirect taxes also increase their share of total output significantly, a fact which is clearly evidenced from the table.

CHAPTER 7

C O N C L U S I O N S

The preliminary findings and, indeed, some of the conclusive observations have already been made in Chapter 1 in the discussion of "An Overview of Research Findings." It should, therefore, prove useful to refer to that section where the total Jamaican situation, as it relates to the study, is vividly assessed and put in sharp focus.

Those findings that are most illuminating and most critical to the development process will, however, be re-emphasized here. But this chapter is reserved, more particularly, for the findings and observations of the projections aspect of the study and the caution that should be exercised in their interpretation and implementation.

The study indicates that, as regards growth in real terms, there is a declining secular trend of the Jamaican economy. Seemingly, one of the problems is due to the fact that while mining, utilities and finance have been the most responsive sectors to growth for over a quarter of a century, over the last ten years the viability of mining and utilities has been significantly diminished. Secondly, over the last ten years, too, the vitality of the manufacturing sector, relative to overall economic activity, has also been considerably reduced. Furthermore, while the efforts made during the last ten years to revitalize agriculture did produce positive changes, these changes were not meaningful enough to help in the growth process in a significant way. These problems are coincident with a falling rate of growth of investment from 7.0 to 5.0 percent over this latter period.

The above points to the fact that since there are serious problems in the primary and secondary

107

industries, problems in the economy as a whole are inevitable because the tertiary industries are not developed to the degree where they can adequately serve the needs of the country. Moreover, tourism, the biggest service industry, is characteristically unstable. This suggests that efforts must be made to strengthen the foundations of the primary and secondary sectors if stability in the economy is to be enhanced. But this also suggests that the vibrant transformation which began in the Jamaican economy some time ago has, unfortunately, not been consolidated.[1]

However, if the problems mentioned above are not accentuated and in the absence of any unforeseen difficulties the vigor of the economy can be gradually reinstated. One of the indices of this optimism is the current[2] domestic saving ratio of 16.2[3] percent relative to GNP. This saving ratio has not fallen over the last twenty-five

---

[1] On matters dealing with economic transformation in a society, see for example, Colin Clarke, op. cit.; W. W. Rostow, The Stages of Economic Growth. New York: Cambridge Press, 1960.; W. A. Lewis, "Economic Development with Unlimited Supplies of labor, "The Manchester School", May 1954, pp. 139-191. This famous article is reprinted in The Economics of Underdevelopment, ed. by A. N. Agarwala and S. P. Singh (Fair Lawn, N. J.: Oxford Press, 1958), selection 6.: Studies in Economic Development, ed. by B. Okun and R. W. Richardson (New York: Holt, 1961), selection 24; Readings in Economic Development, ed. by T. Morgan, G. W. Betz, and N. K. Choudhry (Belmont, Calif.; Wadsworth Press, 1963), selection 20.

[2] Words like "current," "recent," etc., should be taken to mean essentially the sample period between 1959 and 1974.

[3] Lewis, op. cit., makes the point that the central problem of economic development is to increase saving from a 4.0 to 5.0 percent of national income to a 12.0 to 15.0 percent.

years, a negative personal saving, notwithstanding.[4] In addition, gross saving, including
inflows from the rest of the world now approximates 23.0 percent and the country has been able
to attract relatively more foreign saving in recent time. Nevertheless, the proper inducement
should be given so that this saving is not expatriated, or diverted to luxurious housing, etc.,
with little or no growth stimulating or growth
promoting properties.

One of the ways in which the long term problems should be solved is by import substitution;
but the evidence tends to suggest that, in the
main, where there was reduction of imports it did
not reflect so much development of these substi-
tute industries as an attempt to minimize balance
of payments problems--not a bad thing in itself.

As far as the projections are concerned, it
should be re-emphasized, firstly, that they are
not meant to be precise predictions of the future
and no claim is made that the projected values set
out in the tables are going to be the actual
values assumed by the economy, necessarily. Nor
does the model pretend to be able to capture all
the refinements of the system such as unexpected
booms or unforeseen catastrophies. What the projections are intended to show, primarily, is the
direction the economy will take and the speed and
degree of the change that can be expected if

---

[4] It is possible that personal saving could become
positive when Jamaicans get adjusted away from their pre-
vious "peak" growth in income which the country experienced
in the past. See M. Friedman, A Theory of the Consumption
Function, Princeton, N.J.: Princeton University Press,
1957. See also T.M. Brown, "Habit Persistence and Consumer
Behavior," Econometrica, vol. 20, July 1952, pp. 355-371.
For questions dealing with the so-called "peak" income, see
J.S. Duesenberry, "Relative Income Hypothesis" in his
Income, Saving and the Theory of Consumer Behavior,
Cambridge, Mass.: Harvard University Press, 1949.

certain variables--in this case the fiscal policy variables--are suitably engineered.

Even then, it must be borne in mind that these projected expected changes are based on the past performance of the economy and assumes no significant change of the structural parameters, except those that have been explicitly varied to effect the desired ends. As pointed out in Chapter 1, this is one of the inherent weaknesses of this type of model expecially for long term projections since they assume no change in the structural coefficients--and structural changes are, indeed, likely in a developing country.

This study, for example, assumes a constant capital-output ratio; but conceivably, this ratio could be reduced and this would speed up growth much more quickly.[5] This, incidentally, appears to be a fruitful area to which energies should be directed. Neither did the production function of this model consider things like technology, economies of scale, investment in human capital, nor managerial capacity, explicity, even though these were not considered especial constraints in this study.[6]

---

[5] For some of the complexities surrounding capital and the capital output ratio see Kindleberger, op. cit., pp. 87-92. See also Walter Heller, "Fiscal Policies for Under-developed Countries in Agricultural Taxation and Economic Development, ed. by H. Wald (Cambridge, Mass,: Harvard University Law School, 1954) esp. p. 62; R. M. Solow, Growth Theory: An Exposition (New York: Oxford University Press, 1970), pp. 17-38.

[6] For the contribution of these variables to the development process, see, for example, Kindleberger, op. cit. In the aggregate sense, and for convenience, economists sometimes tend to treat all these variables as technology and, therefore, as a single factor of production. Moreover, some like Nicholas Kaldor argue that capital and technology cannot be separated since much of technology is embodied in

In spite of these shortcomings--a factor characteristically present in models in one form or
another--this model, along with the projections,
has yielded invaluable insights as to the economic
forces and interrelationships underlying the economy. It is indicated in the previous section,
for example, that if sheer momentum moves the
economy forward without any further decline,
investment requirements will absorb between 23.0
and 24.0 percent of total output each year; and
the public sector will gradually increase its
share of economic activity over time.

However, at the higher rates of growth (Tables 10
and 11), even though these rates are induced
largely by increased taxes directed into capital
formation, it was the private sector which increases its share of output on the demand side.
An implication of this result is that if government is capable of intercepting the resources from
consumption, the business community will put it to
work.

The model and the projection exercise also
throws some light on the gigantic task which lies
ahead and the severe sacrifices which would have
to be made if the higher growth rates are to be
attempted as the economy is presently constituted. Saving, for example, would have to climb
to approximately 39.0 percent of output by 1985 if
the 6.0 percent rate of growth is to be achieved.

According to the consistency values of this
solution (Appendix A.4) the indications are that
for this to be fulfilled, imports of non-food
(Mnf) such as cars, washers, television sets and
the like would have to be halted from 1975 and the
local production of these goods developed gradually to reach a value of $165.50 million by 1985.

The pattern indicated above, is, in fact, the
pattern suggested by all the different levels of
growth above the historical rate, except that the
urgency differs commensurate with the speed of
development involved: consumption, and particularly non-food consumption goods originating from

111

abroad, must be drastically reduced while both capital and intermediate goods imports correspondingly increased. A basic implication of this result is that under the existing Jamaican economic structure, while saving and investment are indispensable for growth, at the higher rates of growth, they are not sufficient. Development of the import substitutes of consumer (and perhaps producer) goods is necessary to achieve a rate of growth above 5.4 percent.[7] Failing this, increased foreign saving or foreign exchange to pay for the necessary imports must be generated either directly through increased capital inflow or indirectly by way of a larger volume of exports. An alternative implication is that it is not economically feasible to escalate the rate of growth in Jamaica to as high as 6.0 percent in real terms as the economy is presently structured.

---

[7] Beginning with this level of growth the simulation solution suggests that import substitutes of non-food consumer goods would have to be forthcoming, starting with $3.70 million in 1978 and gradually increasing thereafter until it attains a value of $73.20 million in 1985.

CHAPTER 8

E P I L O G U E

THE CHANGING TIMES

Since the time this manuscript was conceived, researched and sent to press, a number of things have happened and, perhaps, even a greater number of things have changed. There have been radical changes in Iran; beginning with the closing days of Mr. Nixon and now Mr. Reagan, the American Presidency has changed hands four times; and there have been drastic social and philosophical changes in China, to name a few. All these events have affected to a greater or lesser degree, the internal economies of the countries involved.

The changes alluded to above seem to be the nature of things in the world today; and, what with the developments in communication, transportation, political awareness, and so on, there is no end in sight to this kind of social dynamism.

Jamaica, the focal point of this book, has had its full share of contemporary changes, the most significant of which coincided with the new socialist policy introduced under the PNP government between 1972 and 1980. Indeed, the writing of this Epilogue is, in part, prompted by the severe decline of the Jamaican economy over the recent past. As such, this chapter will re-emphasize some of the limitations of the Klein-type econometric model and how the projections may best be utilized within the context of a changing economic environment.

This Epilogue will also provide a forum to underscore an important fact: although economics is sometimes referred to as the Queen of the

113

Social Sciences, it must rely considerably on the other social sciences if successful programs are to be formulated. Moreover, there is no aspect of economics where this argument is more applicable than in the field of economic development.

A few observations will, accordingly, be made on the problems of economic underdevelopment with special reference to "The Frailty of Open Econo- mies". Similarly, a brief comment will be made, not only on some of the crucial issues in "The Economics of Public Policy" but also on "Mohammed and the Mountain" or how socio-economic policy may be machined to maximize the use of local resources.

UTILITY OF THE PROJECTIONS

The weaknesses of econometric models as they relate to the making of precise future predictions have been amply stated already in chapter 1 and again in chapter 7. Of course, it is to be re- membered that it is not that anything is wrong with the models themselves. Indeed, as a predic- tive device they compare favorably with, and some- times even superior to, other model types.[1] Nor should it be considered that any model is infalli- ble, since the best of them merely represents generalizations about reality.

As has been shown earlier, however, a good, well specified model is capable of making reasona- bly accurate predictions about the future of the economy if the underlying assumptions remain in place. The quality and predictive accuracy of our model has already been duly verified in chapter 6. The real problem then, it may be recalled, is that with these types of models, since they re- flect the structure of the economy for a past period, if the structure changes significantly, so

---

[1] See, for example, Evans, *op.cit.*, pp. 516-530.

114

too will be the values of the predicted variables.

It does not mean, however, that because of probable changes in society these models should not be used. Nor does it mean that research should cease. For what if the contemplated changes do not occur? Then, no time would be lost and a properly specified model would be at hand to use as required by policy makers; or if the model had already been used as a guide to introduce desirable changes, then the society is the beneficiary.

Suppose we assume, for the moment, though, that changes do occur. The model along with the projected variables will now stand ready to provide at least some of the evidence-- perhaps the only objective evidence--as to the factors that are structurally responsible and the degree of their responsibility. If the change is a positive one, more of the same prescription is suggested and there may be no needed change in the policy parameters. But then again, adjustments may be necessary to maintain or "accentuate the positive." If, on the other hand, the economy suffers a decline, again the projected figures stand ready to show the extent to which it must be brought back on course and the sectors that are likely to be the most crucial in making this correction.

It is a matter of record and common knowledge that over the last few years, especially following 1975, the decline in the Jamaican economy has reached catastrophic proportions. It is clear, therefore, that the value of the projected figures contained in this book will far overshoot the present actual figures of the economic variables. But, as was shown above, the projections can now serve as an important guide, indicating where the economy would be in the absence of the changed conditions. In other words, even neglecting the Accelerated rates for the moment, the Historical or Trend rate of growth of 3.90 percent (Appendix A.1) can easily be used to estimate the damage that the economy has sustained. More than this,

115

it can show the overall magnitude of the resources that must be harnessed to return the economy to the "predepressionary" period.

Aside from the total resource that must be assembled for the restoration process, the model also presents us with various options as to how this total may be packaged. It is obvious, however, that because the economy has been depleted in so many ways, a major--perhaps _the_ major--part of the rehabilitation resource must take the form of foreign saving. It is not surprising, therefore, that the new government was quick to enlist the help of the International Monetary Fund (IMF) to secure a loan of three quarters of a billion dollars-- and this is an attempt to close only the foreign exchange gap.[2]

UNDERDEVELOPMENT REVISITED:
THE FRAILTY OF OPEN ECONOMIES

Reference has been made in a very general way in chapter 1 to the characteristics and problems of economic underdevelopment. Among them are the shortage of capital and technology, the relatively high degree of illiteracy, the comparatively high rate of population increase and the problem of disguised unemployment. Here, the problem of trade will be highlighted--even if briefly--since under some circumstances it can play such a prominent role in development.[3] In fact, the impetus to re-examine the foreign trade function stems

---

[2] The Jamaica Weekly Gleaner (North American Edition), February 16, 1981.

[3] See, for example, Kindleberger, _op. cit._, PP. 295-321. Simon Kuznets even argues that "Small countries can attain economic growth only through heavy reliance on foreign trade". Kuznets, _op. cit_., Chapter 6, particularly p. 302.

116

from the decided role it played over the last few years in the Jamaican economy--the focus of the empirical aspect of this book. The overall impact was not only contributory to a deceleration of growth but, ultimately, a reversal of some of the gains that had been made previously.

One of the main disadvantages of less developed countries is that they usually have one or a few basic export commodities. When prices fluctuate in world markets--as they usually do--this has a correspondingly adverse effect on growth. Moreover, since these exports are likely to be primary products, the long-run demand for them tends to fall in preference to manufactured goods and luxuries.[4] This is in keeping with the well known Engel's Law.

Primary products also tend to be over supplied at times; and being inclined to be inelastic as well, they are usually subject to adverse terms of trade with their manufactured goods counterpart from industrial regions.[5] Because of these general problems many authorities argue in favor of the flexibility that diversification offers, rather that "slavishly" specializing in the few goods or industries that classical comparative advantage suggests.[6] At the very least, a _prima facie_ case can be made supporting the merits of this contention.

---

[4] Many observers on international trade issues point to this problem. See, for example, Kindleberger, _op.cit._, pp. 298-307.

[5] This once controversal point is becoming more accepted. See, for example, Kindleberger, _op. cit._, pp. 297-300. In his work on Jamaica, Jeffreyson finds the commodity terms of trade to be decidedly unfavorable to Jamaica. Jeffreyson, _op. cit._ pp. 200-202.

[6] Standard texts on economics generally reserve a space to air the controversy between trade specialization or

117

On the other side of the coin, the imports are equally critical in the process of development--and in many respects even more so. Indeed, the anxiety about exports is largely because they must provide the foreign exchange necessary to pay for these imports in the absence of foreign saving. If the inflow of capital and raw materials used in the various enterprises is jeopardized, the growth machinery is essentially stalled. It is in view of this potential danger why import substitution is so strongly recommended in chapter 7. This, incidentally, is also consistent with the "diversification thesis" cited above.

The picture painted by the foregoing arguments suggests that since open economies must rely quite substantially on their foreign trade sector for their overall economic activity, they can be easily influenced by external forces. This sentiment is explicitly suggested in the model in making export of goods (Xg) an exogenous factor. However, the problem will not normally be as acute for developed economies as for less developed ones. In general, the developed countries are likely to have a more diversified set of export industries over which the risks of failure can be spread. They are also usually more self sufficient in capital and other manufactured goods. As shown above, the converse is true for the underdeveloped economies and, as such, they make very "frail specimens of open economies."

Based on the preceeding discussion, a similar

---

diversification. Most of the arguments, however, seem to lean towards diversification either to achieve "balanced growth", to reap "the fruits of industrialization", to gain the benefits of "import substitution", or to receive the advantages of "export promotion". See, for example, Kindleberger, op. cit., pp. 213-225; 296-313; Samuelson, op. cit., pp. 719-720.

argument can also be applied from the import side. Underdeveloped economies also make frail specimens of open economies because, unlike (many) developed economies, their import substitution industries, where they exist, are not usually developed to the degree where they can accommodate crisis situations when they occur. Furthermore, since they are poorer, they do not have the same capacity to borrow from foreign sources.

In the light of these realities, it is imperative that, as a practical matter, the trading and economic relationships of a less developed country like Jamaica, for example, get more than passing interest. It could spell the difference between a move towards prosperity or a drift to retrogression. Attention is, therefore, turned to some of these very issues in the next section.

ECONOMICS OF PUBLIC POLICY

Whether government should play an active or passive role in economic development remains a lively debate. Perhaps this is how it should be because there are examples of countries in which economic growth flourishes as well as fails under either situation. Moreover, a given country may pursue a passive or active government policy as circumstances warrant. Government's role in America, for example, was comparatively passive before the Great Depression but evolved in a significantly active one thereafter, giving credence, in the meantime, to the concept of the "Mixed Economy". Currently, President Reagan feels that the national interest will be best served by reducing the present size of the public sector.

Given the contemporary state of global political economy, public policy is poised to play a crucial role, perhaps, like capital and technology, in the process of economic development. For one, what with the spread of education, communication and nationalism in Third World countries, their governments are likely to remain or become increasingly more active. Furthermore, their efforts are now institutionalized and articulated through the New International Economic Order (NIEO). Secondly, governments are inclined to grow as development progresses. Thirdly, the cold war between "East" and "West" has intensified in recent time and polarization may intensify as well. Fourthly, economic warfare is a more humane and attractive alternative than conventional guns and bombs.

Since public policy for any country must have economic development as one of its national objectives, policy makers cannot be oblivious of these contingencies. For a developing country where economic growth is not only an important objective but a national priority, it is even more imperative that the choice of public policy is pragmatic enough to reflect these realities.

A responsive public policy will also mean other things as well. It cannot neglect the country's history, culture, or sociological character. Any sharp break with the past in all these areas is a certain way to court disaster, since neither producer nor consumer will be able to cope with these sudden changes.

Another common problem in public policy is an attempt to "short circuit" the development and growth process. These terms in themselves imply passage of time and should remind us that true prosperity cannot be achieved overnight. The simple reason is that the more of the resources divided up as consumer goods now, the less must remain as producer goods. The paradox here is that while it is politically glamorous to attempt instant prosperity for all, it usually means affluence for none.

Short circuiting the growth process should not be confused with a rapid rate of growth where there is the necessary economic base. It means trying to move from a state of poverty to a state of prosperity without a period of capital accumulation. It is in this area that Karl Marx is, perhaps, most misunderstood and misinterpreted by many an over zealous policy maker.

Much of Jamaica's problems, accentuated since 1975, can be traced to some or all of these issues. Any serious attempt to revitalize the economy, therefore, will have to include the choice of an overall public policy which does not disregard the social, cultural, political and economic norms that have already been institution-alized. When, for example, true patriotic Jamai-can nationals become skeptical and begin to emi-grate with their capital and technology as a result, foreign investors cannot help but see this as a negative cue. No capital and technology, no growth. Simple.

MOHAMMED AND THE MOUNTAIN

In the last section, a strong implication was made that the development process could be seri-ously jeopardized or retarded if the social and cultural under-pinnings of the society are ne-glected. Some have even said these factors are pre-eminent compared with the economic.[7] Even if we do not support the primacy of the non-economic factors, their significance is unques-tionable. The well-known story is told of the expert from a developed economy who, with the best of intentions, formulated a program to increase the protein in the diet of the Indian people. His approach was to increase the cattle population. As the story goes, the cattle population exploded but the program was defeated because, as a rule, the Indian people do not eat beef.

The moral of this story is clear. A lot of time, energy and resources can be wasted in the absence of the socio-cultural input. Based on this analogy, a country's rate of development

---

[7] See, for example, Kindleberger, op.cit., pp. 18-39.

could be considerably diminished if due recognition is not given to those traditions that are accepted and those that are rejected. Most societies, for example, seem to reject at least some part of their colonial past--usually that part which is associated with defamation such as slavery.

Conversely, that part of a colonial past associated with high status is usually accepted like, for example, white collar jobs. Indeed, one of the problems of less developed economies--and even in many developed ones as well--is underemployment in agricultural enterprises. And this is so even when the wage compares favorably with industrial jobs.

When, therefore, because of social traditions a people refuse to do certain jobs, thus worsening the unemployment situation, one of the strategies in development should be to pursue those industries which will voluntarily engage large quantities of the labor force. In other words, since disguised unemployment and underemployment constitute too heavy a cost for any economy to bear, if large numbers of the population refuse to accept certain occupations, opportunities for other positions should be created for them. In this respect the relationship is like the "mountain going to Mohammed" rather than the reverse.

In Jamaica, for example, a large part of the labor force refuses or is hesitant to work in agriculture, in general, and sugar canes in particular--even where the wage is competitive. Persons in the same group will happily work in a manufacturing environment. Even more interesting is the fact that many of these same workers show little resistance to work in sugar canes in Florida, U.S.A. Perhaps this is so because America is not only removed from the local scene but, also, because it is more egalitarian.

While it is true that education can be used to promote the dignity of all work, sometimes this fails or produces only limited success. Accordingly, enterprises should be considered to maximize the use of labor at the margin with the other factors of production. Bringing _meaningful_ occupations to the workers is important because in the absence of an abundance of capital and technology it is a sure way of enhancing economic growth. But it is also a means of achieving another important national objective--that of improving income distribution.

APPENDIX

Appendix A.I. Model Solution and Projection of Economic Variables at 3.9 percent growth: 1974-86

						Exogenous Variable					Endogenous				Variable	
C	Pop	D	ETrs	Kt-1	In	Xg	Xfs	Trb	Trg	Trmg	Trg	Trml	Trxp	Srml	K	Y
535.8	202.5	1.0	577.8	1998.4	2.8	236.2	1.3	17.1	0.7	10.2	9.3	18.5	19.6	40.5	2182.7	
540.3	205.5	1.0	602.0	2182.7	8.0	249.0	14.4	19.4	1.2	11.0	8.8	20.3	24.5	65.9	2346.5	845.3

	1974	1975	1976	1977	1978	1979	1980	1981	1982	1983	1984	1985
Mc	540.3	555.5	570.8	587.9	606.0	625.1	645.1	665.8	687.4	709.8	733.1	757.3
C	111.5	118.7	124.7	131.7	138.9	146.5	154.3	162.5	170.9	179.7	188.9	198.4
A	383.9	425.4	444.1	465.2	487.3	510.5	534.8	560.4	587.2	615.3	644.8	675.8
Pf	40.2	41.5	42.4	43.5	44.6	45.7	46.9	48.2	49.5	50.9	52.3	53.7
Pmf	54.1	53.7	53.6	52.8	52.4	52.2	52.4	52.8	53.5	54.4	55.7	57.3
Ma	82.8	97.3	100.8	105.2	109.6	114.0	118.6	123.4	128.3	133.4	138.7	144.3
Mis	129.7	140.6	150.3	161.0	173.2	185.4	198.1	211.2	224.8	239.0	253.7	269.0
Mfs	36.0	50.5	54.0	58.4	62.7	67.2	71.8	76.6	81.5	86.6	92.0	97.5
Mos	37.8	38.7	39.5	40.4	41.4	42.4	43.5	44.0	45.7	46.9	48.2	49.4
Me	97.6	98.3	99.4	99.6	100.3	101.4	102.9	104.7	106.8	109.3	112.2	115.6
Rm	144.8	154.9	162.7	171.7	181.0	190.8	200.9	211.5	222.5	233.9	245.7	258.0
Te	22.5	22.3	22.4	22.3	22.4	22.2	22.1	22.1	22.0	22.0	21.9	21.9
Tc	30.0	31.7	33.3	35.1	37.1	39.0	41.1	43.2	45.5	47.8	50.2	52.7
Tgi	27.7	29.5	31.2	33.1	35.1	37.2	39.3	41.6	43.9	46.3	48.8	51.4
Tsg	0.5	0.8	0.8	0.8	0.8	0.8	0.8	0.8	0.8	0.7	0.7	0.7
TB	51.8	55.8	59.0	62.8	66.7	70.8	75.1	79.5	84.1	88.9	93.9	99.1
TTP	37.1	40.4	42.8	45.6	48.5	51.5	54.6	57.9	61.3	64.8	68.5	72.3
Tau	9.1	9.7	10.3	10.9	11.5	12.1	12.8	13.5	14.3	15.0	15.8	16.6
S	166.6	198.9	205.8	214.3	222.7	231.4	240.4	249.6	259.3	269.3	279.6	290.4
Ssp	33.4	36.2	36.0	40.0	42.1	44.3	46.6	49.0	51.5	54.1	56.8	59.6
Sp	-20.4	-21.9	-24.3	-26.3	-28.7	-31.4	-34.3	-37.3	-40.4	-43.6	-47.0	-50.6
Sd	51.4	54.4	56.4	59.7	62.7	65.8	69.0	72.3	75.8	79.4	83.2	87.1
Sd	61.7	64.2	67.1	70.0	73.1	76.3	79.7	83.1	86.7	90.4	94.3	98.4
π	107.4	114.6	120.2	126.9	133.8	141.1	148.6	156.4	164.6	173.0	181.8	190.9
y	812.7	845.3	874.3	908.1	943.1	979.5	1017.3	1056.7	1097.5	1139.9	1184.0	1229.7
Ym	645.3	671.1	691.4	715.4	740.3	766.3	793.4	821.6	850.8	881.2	912.7	945.4
Yp	517.3	599.7	615.8	634.7	654.4	675.0	696.4	718.6	741.7	765.6	790.5	816.4
Yd	340.2	559.3	573.0	589.2	606.0	623.5	641.7	660.7	680.4	700.8	722.1	744.1
Yrs	349.2	364.8	378.7	394.8	411.5	429.0	447.0	465.8	485.4	505.6	526.7	548.6
I	166.0	198.9	205.8	214.3	222.7	231.4	240.4	249.6	259.3	269.3	279.6	290.4
Ifp	29.6	31.4	32.8	34.5	36.2	37.9	39.8	41.7	43.7	45.8	47.9	50.2
X	163.8	191.0	197.5	205.7	213.8	222.2	230.8	239.7	248.9	258.5	268.5	278.8
Xs	343.0	361.5	374.0	396.5	416.0	436.4	457.9	480.5	504.2	529.1	555.3	582.8
Xs	107.4	112.5	115.6	120.0	124.5	129.2	134.1	139.2	144.5	150.0	155.7	161.6
Srp	134.2	159.5	164.7	171.2	177.7	184.2	191.0	198.0	205.2	212.7	220.5	228.7

STATEMENTS EXECUTED= 9119

125

Appendix A.2. Model Solution and Projection of Economic Variables at 4.5 percent growth: 1974-85

Exogenous Variables (best-effort reading)

Year	C	POP	D	ETus	K-1	In	Xf	Tn	Tf1	Tf	Tmf	Tmg	Trsg	Trsh	Snmh	K	Y
1973	535.8	202.5	1.0	577.8	1998.4	2.8	236.2	1.3	17.1	0.7	10.2	9.3	18.5	19.6	40.5	2182.7	845.3
1974	531.3	205.5	1.0	602.6	2182.7	8.0	249.6	14.4	19.4	1.2	11.0	8.8	20.3	24.5	65.9	2376.3	879.6
1975	545.0	208.6	1.0	628.6	2376.3	8.3	262.4	15.0	20.2	1.3	11.4	9.1	21.1	25.5	68.6	2600.5	919.3
1976	560.1	211.8	1.0	655.6	2600.5	8.7	276.6	15.6	21.1	1.3	12.0	9.6	22.1	26.7	71.7	2835.6	960.9
1977	578.7	214.9	1.0	683.8	2835.6	9.1	291.5	16.3	22.1	1.3	12.5	10.0	23.1	27.9	74.9	3082.5	1004.6
1978	599.3	218.2	1.0	713.2	3082.5	9.5	307.2	17.1	23.1	1.4	13.1	10.4	24.1	29.1	78.4	3341.6	1050.4
1979	621.5	221.4	1.0	743.8	3341.1	9.9	323.8	17.5	24.2	1.5	13.7	10.9	25.2	30.5	81.9	3611.6	1098.2
1980	644.9	224.7	1.0	775.8	3611.6	10.3	341.3	18.7	25.3	1.5	14.3	11.4	26.4	31.8	85.7	3894.5	1148.3
1981	669.6	228.1	1.0	809.2	3894.5	10.8	355.8	19.5	26.4	1.6	14.9	11.9	27.6	33.3	89.6	4190.1	1200.6
1982	695.4	231.5	1.0	844.0	4190.1	11.3	379.2	20.4	27.6	1.7	15.6	12.5	28.8	34.8	93.6	4499.1	1255.3
1983	722.5	235.0	1.0	880.3	4495.1	11.8	399.7	21.3	28.9	1.7	16.3	13.1	30.1	36.4	97.9	4822.1	1312.5
1984	750.8	238.5	1.0	918.1	4822.1	12.4	421.2	22.3	30.2	1.8	17.1	13.6	31.5	38.1	102.4	5159.6	1372.5
1985	780.3	242.1	1.0	957.6	5159.6	12.9	444.0	23.3	31.6	1.9	17.8	14.3	32.9	39.8	107.0	5512.3	

Endogenous Variables (best-effort reading)

	1974	1975	1976	1977	1978	1979	1980	1981	1982	1983	1984	1985
C	533.3	545.0	560.1	578.7	599.3	621.5	644.9	669.6	695.4	722.5	750.8	780.3
Ĉ	72.7	78.2	83.5	89.7	96.2	103.1	110.3	117.9	125.8	134.0	142.6	151.7
H	383.9	424.4	444.1	466.3	489.7	514.3	540.2	567.4	596.1	626.2	657.8	691.0
Mf	39.6	40.8	41.8	43.0	44.3	45.6	47.1	48.6	50.1	51.8	53.5	55.2
Mf'	28.3	24.1	19.6	14.7	10.4	6.2	2.0	-2.1	-6.2	-10.3	-14.4	-18.5
Mk	98.7	115.1	120.9	127.2	133.5	139.8	146.4	153.2	160.4	167.8	175.6	183.7
Mg	129.7	140.6	152.0	165.3	179.2	193.8	209.1	225.1	241.8	259.3	277.6	296.7
Mfs	51.9	68.3	74.1	80.4	86.7	93.1	99.6	106.5	113.6	121.1	128.9	137.0
Mor	37.8	38.7	39.6	40.7	41.9	43.1	44.4	45.8	47.2	48.6	50.2	51.8
Md	65.7	61.7	57.4	52.6	48.4	44.5	40.6	36.9	33.1	29.4	25.6	21.9
Rn	140.6	150.1	158.7	168.7	179.4	190.6	202.3	214.6	227.5	241.0	255.1	269.8
Tc	22.5	22.3	22.2	21.9	21.5	21.1	20.7	20.3	19.8	19.4	18.9	18.3
Te	30.0	31.7	33.6	35.8	38.0	40.4	42.9	45.5	48.2	51.1	54.1	57.2
Tai	27.7	29.5	31.5	33.8	36.1	38.6	41.2	44.0	46.8	49.0	52.9	56.2
Tyg	0.5	0.8	0.8	0.8	0.8	0.8	0.8	0.8	0.7	0.7	0.7	0.7
Tb	49.2	52.9	56.5	60.8	65.3	70.1	75.2	80.5	86.0	91.8	97.9	104.2
TFa	35.4	38.5	41.1	44.3	47.6	51.2	54.9	58.8	62.9	67.2	71.6	76.3
Tbu	9.1	9.7	10.3	11.1	11.8	12.6	13.4	14.3	15.2	16.1	17.1	18.1
Ss	196.4	232.2	243.3	255.6	267.7	280.0	292.7	306.0	319.8	334.3	349.1	365.1
Sf	68.0	71.9	75.2	79.0	83.1	87.5	92.0	96.8	101.8	107.0	112.4	118.1
Sb	-21.3	-22.6	-23.4	-24.9	-27.3	-30.2	-33.4	-36.9	-40.6	-44.4	-48.5	-52.7
Sd	49.5	52.3	55.0	58.2	61.6	65.2	69.1	73.0	77.2	81.6	86.2	90.9
Sd'	61.7	64.7	68.0	71.5	75.2	79.1	83.2	87.4	91.9	96.5	101.3	106.4
F	103.0	109.5	115.8	123.4	131.4	139.0	148.8	158.1	167.8	178.1	188.7	199.9
Y	412.7	845.3	879.6	919.3	960.9	1004.6	1050.4	1098.2	1148.3	1200.6	1255.3	1312.5
Ya	429.4	652.9	675.5	702.6	731.5	761.9	794.0	827.5	862.6	899.4	937.8	977.9
Yp	565.8	586.6	604.6	626.0	648.5	673.0	698.3	724.9	752.6	781.7	812.0	843.8
Yd	510.3	548.1	563.4	581.8	601.2	621.0	643.4	666.1	689.7	714.5	740.4	767.5
Yos	349.2	364.6	381.2	400.2	420.1	441.0	462.8	485.7	509.7	534.7	560.8	588.1
I	196.4	232.2	243.3	255.6	267.7	280.0	280.0	306.0	319.8	334.3	349.3	365.1
Tig	28.8	30.5	32.1	33.9	35.9	37.9	40.1	42.3	44.6	47.1	49.6	52.3
Ti	193.6	224.2	235.0	246.9	258.6	270.5	282.9	295.7	309.0	322.9	337.5	352.7
X	343.6	360.5	377.6	396.8	417.0	438.3	460.8	484.4	509.3	535.4	562.9	591.8
Xs	107.4	111.5	115.2	120.2	125.5	131.1	137.0	143.1	149.5	156.2	163.2	170.6
Ti'	164.8	193.7	202.5	213.0	222.7	232.6	242.8	253.4	264.4	275.9	287.9	300.4

STATEMENTS EXECUTED= 9119

Appendix A.3. Model Solution and Projection of Economic Variables at 5.4 percent growth: 1974-85

	Pop	D	Eiu	Ki-1	In	Xf	Xis	Tb	Fri	Tnf	Fni	Fri	Trb	Trb	Tryp	Sumh	K	Y
	535.8	202.5	1.0	577.8	1998.4	2.8	236.2	249.0	1.3	17.1	10.2	9.3	18.5	19.6	40.5	2182.7	845.3	
	532.0	205.5	1.0	602.6	2182.7	8.0	249.0	14.4	19.4	11.0	8.8	20.3	24.5	115.8	2382.1			

	1974	1975	1976	1977	1978	1979	1980	1981	1982	1983	1984	1985
C	532.0	533.7	544.0	562.4	585.1	610.8	638.6	668.5	700.2	733.7	769.2	806.7
C	65.1	68.5	73.3	79.8	86.9	94.5	102.5	111.0	120.0	129.5	139.5	150.1
M	303.9	474.0	494.7	521.3	549.3	579.2	610.7	644.0	679.2	716.3	755.4	796.7
Mf	39.5	39.8	40.7	42.0	43.5	45.1	46.8	48.7	50.6	52.6	54.8	57.1
Mn	23.3	24.4	15.5	5.3	-3.7	-12.6	-21.7	-31.1	-40.9	-51.1	-61.9	-73.2
M	101.8	139.8	148.5	158.9	168.7	178.6	189.0	199.8	211.1	223.1	235.7	248.9
Mig	129.7	140.6	152.4	168.4	185.3	203.4	222.6	242.9	264.4	287.0	310.9	336.1
Mls	55.0	93.0	101.8	112.1	121.9	131.9	142.2	153.1	164.4	176.6	189.0	202.3
Mls	37.8	38.7	39.7	41.0	42.4	43.9	45.6	47.3	49.0	50.9	52.9	55.1
Rc	59.5	62.1	52.3	40.9	31.0	21.2	11.3	1.0	-9.8	-21.1	-33.1	-45.7
Rn	139.4	143.5	151.5	162.6	174.8	187.9	201.8	216.5	232.0	248.5	265.8	284.0
Te	22.5	22.3	22.1	21.5	20.7	19.9	19.0	18.0	16.9	15.8	14.6	13.2
Tie	30.0	31.7	33.7	36.3	39.0	42.0	45.1	48.4	51.7	55.6	59.5	63.6
Tii	27.7	29.5	31.6	34.3	37.2	40.3	43.5	47.0	50.7	54.5	58.6	62.4
Tfg	0.5	0.8	0.8	0.8	0.8	0.8	0.8	0.7	0.7	0.7	0.7	0.7
Tb	48.8	49.0	52.2	57.0	62.2	67.9	73.9	80.4	87.2	94.4	102.0	110.0
Typ	35.1	35.8	38.2	41.8	45.6	49.9	54.1	59.1	64.1	69.5	75.1	81.1
Tsu	9.1	9.7	10.4	11.2	12.1	13.1	14.1	15.2	16.4	17.6	18.9	20.3
S	202.2	278.4	295.1	314.9	333.8	353.0	372.8	393.6	415.5	438.5	462.8	488.3
Sg	74.7	75.0	18.2	82.8	87.9	93.4	99.2	105.5	112.0	119.0	126.3	134.0
Si	-23.8	-26.6	-24.2	-23.5	-22.2	-28.1	-31.7	-35.7	-40.1	-44.8	-49.8	-55.1
Sd	49.1	44.3	51.7	55.3	59.2	63.5	68.1	73.0	78.1	83.5	89.3	95.4
	61.7	64.7	68.8	73.1	77.7	82.6	87.7	93.1	98.9	104.9	111.3	118.1
Tr	102.1	102.4	108.2	116.0	125.8	135.8	146.5	157.9	169.9	182.6	196.0	210.2
Y	812.7	845.3	880.6	928.5	979.2	1033.4	1090.9	1151.6	1215.8	1283.5	1355.1	1430.5
Ym	626.3	628.1	648.1	678.3	711.5	747.5	786.0	826.8	870.1	915.7	964.0	1015.0
Yp	563.5	584.7	584.7	608.9	635.3	663.9	694.5	726.9	761.2	797.5	835.8	876.2
Yd	528.4	532.8	546.5	567.1	589.7	614.1	640.1	667.8	697.0	728.0	760.6	795.1
Yss	347.2	364.8	381.7	404.6	428.8	454.7	482.2	511.2	541.9	574.3	608.5	644.6
H	202.2	278.4	295.1	314.9	333.8	353.0	372.8	393.6	415.5	438.5	462.8	488.3
Iff	28.7	29.3	30.8	32.8	35.0	37.4	39.9	42.6	45.5	48.4	51.6	54.9
	199.4	270.4	286.8	306.2	324.5	343.2	362.6	382.8	404.0	426.4	450.0	474.9
X	343.6	360.3	376.1	390.3	417.5	440.1	463.9	489.0	515.5	543.5	573.0	604.1
Xs	107.4	111.3	113.7	119.7	126.0	132.8	140.0	147.7	155.8	164.3	173.4	182.9
Kpr	110.7	241.0	256.0	273.3	289.5	305.8	322.6	340.2	358.6	378.0	398.4	419.9

STATEMENTS EXECUTED= 9119

Appendix A.4. Model Solution and Projection of Economic Variables at 6.0 percent growth: 1974-85

Exogenous Variables

Var.	1974	1975	1976	1977	1978	1979	1980	1981	1982	1983	1984	1985
C	535.8	490.9	473.8	475.1	488.1	508.1	531.5	557.7	586.2	616.7	649.2	683.9 720.8
POP	202.5	205.5	208.6	211.8	214.9	218.2	221.4	224.7	228.1	231.5	235.0	238.5 242.1
D	1.0	1.0	1.0	1.0	1.0	1.0	1.0	1.0	1.0	1.0	1.0	1.0
ETus	577.8	602.6	628.6	655.6	683.8	713.2	743.8	775.8	809.2	844.0	880.3	918.1 957.6
Ki-1	1998.4	2182.7	2398.5	2697.6	3020.7	3369.3	3741.7	4138.5	4560.5	5009.0	5485.6	5991.9 6529.7
In	2.8	8.0	8.3	8.8	9.4	9.9	10.6	11.2	11.9	12.1	13.5	14.3 15.2
X9	236.2	249.0	262.4	276.6	291.5	307.2	323.8	341.3	359.8	379.2	399.7	421.2 444.0
Xis	1.3	14.4	15.0	15.9	16.9	17.9	19.1	20.3	21.5	22.9	24.3	25.8 27.5
Trp	17.1	19.4	20.3	21.5	22.9	24.3	25.8	27.4	29.1	30.9	32.9	34.9 37.1
Trs	0.7	1.2	1.2	1.3	1.4	1.5	1.6	1.7	1.8	1.9	2.0	2.1 2.3
Trmf	10.2	11.0	11.5	12.2	12.9	13.7	14.6	15.5	16.5	17.5	18.6	19.8 21.0
Txt	9.3	8.8	9.2	9.7	10.3	11.0	11.7	12.4	13.2	14.0	14.9	15.8 16.8
Trmt	18.5	20.3	21.2	22.5	23.8	25.3	26.9	28.6	30.4	32.3	34.3	36.5 38.8
Tsmb	19.6	24.5	25.6	27.2	28.8	30.6	32.5	34.6	36.7	39.0	41.5	44.1 46.8
K	40.5	115.8	121.0	128.3	136.1	144.6	153.6	163.2	173.5	184.3	195.9	208.2 221.2
Y	2182.7	2398.5	2697.6	3020.7	3369.3	3741.7	4138.5	4560.5	5009.0	5485.6	5991.9	6529.7 7100.9

Endogenous Variables

Var.	1974	1975	1976	1977	1978	1979	1980	1981	1982	1983	1984	1985
G	490.9	473.8	475.1	488.1	508.1	531.5	557.7	586.2	616.7	649.2	683.9	720.8
M	81.0	84.2	89.8	97.9	106.1	116.5	126.9	138.0	149.8	162.3	175.6	189.8
Mf	383.9	473.5	494.5	522.2	551.8	583.5	617.1	652.8	690.6	730.7	773.0	817.9
Ml	9.1	-0.9	-16.9	-32.9	-47.4	-61.9	-76.8	-92.5	-109.1	-126.7	-145.5	-165.5
Ma	110.6	155.1	167.9	181.5	194.3	207.2	220.7	234.9	249.9	265.7	282.6	300.4
Mfg	129.7	140.6	153.3	171.0	190.1	210.8	232.8	256.2	281.2	307.7	335.9	365.9
Mfs	63.8	108.3	121.2	134.7	147.5	160.5	174.0	188.2	203.2	219.1	235.9	253.8
Mos	37.8	38.7	39.7	41.2	42.8	44.4	46.4	48.4	50.5	52.7	55.0	57.8
Mc	42.0	30.8	12.3	-6.3	-23.0	-39.6	-56.8	-74.9	-94.1	-114.5	-136.4	-159.8
Rm	195.6	198.7	208.8	224.1	241.1	259.8	279.8	301.2	324.0	348.2	373.8	401.1
Tc	19.0	18.7	18.2	17.0	15.7	14.3	12.7	11.0	9.1	7.1	4.9	2.5
Tci	42.5	44.9	47.6	51.4	55.5	59.9	64.6	69.7	75.0	80.7	86.8	93.2
Tig	62.6	65.9	69.7	75.0	80.7	86.9	93.5	100.5	108.0	115.9	124.3	133.3
T3	0.5	0.8	0.8	0.8	0.8	0.8	0.7	0.7	0.7	0.7	0.7	0.6
Trp	48.1	46.8	49.8	55.0	60.9	67.5	74.7	82.3	90.5	99.1	108.4	118.2
T4u	45.0	44.9	44.9	51.2	55.8	60.8	66.2	72.1	78.3	84.9	91.9	99.4
Sp	6.7	7.2	7.8	8.6	9.4	10.3	11.3	12.4	13.5	14.7	16.0	17.3
Sg	218.6	307.1	331.4	357.3	381.8	406.7	432.6	459.8	488.5	519.0	551.3	585.6
Sb	114.6	114.5	119.0	126.2	134.3	143.3	152.9	163.2	174.2	185.8	198.2	211.3
Sd	-40.8	-29.9	-21.7	-18.4	-19.0	-21.4	-24.8	-28.8	-33.3	-38.1	-43.3	-48.8
Ty	42.5	41.7	43.6	47.0	50.8	55.1	59.7	64.7	70.0	75.6	81.6	88.0
Yn	61.7	65.0	69.5	74.3	79.5	85.1	91.1	97.4	104.1	111.3	118.9	127.0
Yp	86.8	84.9	89.3	97.2	106.2	116.2	127.0	138.8	150.9	164.1	178.1	192.9
Yd	84.9	845.3	883.5	936.5	993.7	1055.3	1116.2	1191.5	1266.2	1345.6	1429.9	1519.5
Yss	812.7	564.1	580.2	608.5	640.9	676.9	715.7	757.4	801.8	849.1	899.4	952.9
H	571.0	515.5	527.5	549.7	575.1	603.0	633.1	665.6	700.2	736.9	776.0	817.5
Tfg	515.5	469.6	480.3	490.5	519.3	542.2	567.0	593.6	621.9	652.0	684.0	718.1
Ir	470.4	364.8	383.1	408.4	435.7	465.2	496.7	530.3	566.0	603.9	644.1	687.1
Xs	349.2	307.1	331.4	357.3	381.8	406.7	432.6	459.8	488.5	519.0	551.3	585.6
Ixm	218.0	39.4	41.2	44.0	47.1	50.5	54.2	58.1	62.2	66.6	71.3	76.2
	38.8	299.1	323.1	348.5	372.5	396.8	422.0	448.5	476.6	506.3	537.8	571.3
	215.8	359.7	375.5	396.1	418.1	441.4	466.2	492.5	520.2	549.6	580.6	613.3
	343.6	110.8	113.1	119.6	126.5	134.2	142.4	151.1	160.5	170.4	180.9	192.1
	107.4	259.7	281.9	304.5	326.4	346.3	367.8	390.5	414.4	439.7	466.5	495.0
	177.0											

STATEMENTS EXECUTED= 9119

128

Appendix B. Ex post Forecast of Non-food: 1959-74

PLOT OF ACTUAL(*) AND FITTED(+) VALUES

PLOT OF RESIDUALS(0)

ACTUAL	FITTED	DATE	RESIDUAL
482.0	506.7	M59	-24.7
574.0	573.5	60	.469
504.0	499.9	61	4.10
460.0	463.9	62	-3.87
506.0	501.8	63	4.23
618.0	624.4	64	-6.40
550.0	550.2	65	-.230
518.6	531.4	66	-12.8
375.6	371.0	67	4.64
422.8	410.3	68	12.0
504.9	470.3	69	34.6
493.0	469.7	70	23.3
471.3	460.2	71	11.0
531.6	530.1	72	1.55
408.5	411.7	73	-3.23
350.0	394.8	74	-44.8
		75	
		76	
		77	

Appendix C. Solution Matrices of Endogenous (A) and Exogenous (B) Variables

Appendix 4. Estimates and Identities of the Overall Model

$\mathcal{A}$. Quantitative Estimates of Equation (22)

						R^2	D. W.
1.	C	=	39.3281 (1.3986)	+	$0.7081Y_d + 0.3675C_{t-1}$ $(4.1733) \quad (2.5035$	0.968	2.8141
2.	G	=	-32.4364 (-3.0273)	+	$0.3368R_n + 0.1171Y$ $(4.0672) \quad (4.2529)$	0.966	1.2920
3.	Xs	=	-85.8180 $(-2.6729$	+	$0.3288Y - 0.0338 \sum_{i=0}^{n} I_{fi}$ $(4.7432) \quad (-2.7432)$	0.881	1.2020
4.	Mf	=	4.59507 (0.8382)	+	$0.0662Y_d$ (5.3762)	0.674	1.2967
5.	Mnf	=	38.9014 (4.4915)	+	$0.8086M_c - 0.3147Pop$ $(11.8461) \quad (-7.9440$	0.935	0.8286
6.	Mk	=	4.63636 (0.4131)	+	$0.5342I_f$ (6.3283)	0.741	1.9310
7.	Mig	=	-114.429 (-6.2643)	+	$0.6993Y_{5s}$ (10.0748)	0.879	0.4830
8.	Mfs	=	$(-5.27262$ (-0.5324)	+	$1.0011M_k - 41.6424D_1$ $(4.6316) \quad (4.0298)$	0.627	2.0530
9.	Mos	=	15.0058 (4.2169)	+	$0.0277Y$ (4.9102)	0.633	1.2840
10.	Tc	=	24.4327 (13.0538)	−	$0.0897Y_{5s} + 0.0505ETUS$ $(-2.8918) \quad (3.1629)$	0.452	0.9342
11.	Te	=	-9.86237 (-2.6007)	+	$0.1135Y_{5s}$ (7.8775)	0.816	1.0138
12.	Toi	=	$(-18.6475$ (-2.4446)	+	$0.0569Y$ (4.7128)	0.613	1.3910
13.	Tb	=	-9.15675 (-1.7530)	+	0.5669 (7.7439)	0.811	1.4149

131

				R^2	D. W.

14. Typ $= \begin{array}{c} -47.7457 \\ (-5.0309) \end{array} + \begin{array}{c} 0.1468Yp \\ (7.2207) \end{array}$ 0.788   0.7627

15. Tsu $= \begin{array}{c} -5.48677 \\ (-3.2022) \end{array} + \begin{array}{c} 0.0176Y \\ (6.4769) \end{array}$ 0.750   1.2997

16. Tyg $= \begin{array}{c} 1.0988 \\ (3.8768) \end{array} + \begin{array}{cc} 0.7769Trg - 0.0014Y \\ (3.7833) \quad (-2.6198) \end{array}$ 0.530   1.5079

17. Sb $= \begin{array}{c} 5.3877 \\ (1.0925) \end{array} + \begin{array}{c} 0.4251 \\ (6.1501) \end{array}$ 0.730   1.3817

18. Pr $= \begin{array}{c} -71.9699 \\ (-4.8186 \end{array} + \begin{array}{c} 0.2776\,Yn \\ (9.4173) \end{array}$ 0.864   1.6660

19. Sd $= \begin{array}{c} 29.0066 \\ (22.4382) \end{array} + \begin{array}{c} 0.0147 \sum_{i=0}^{t} Ifi \\ (12.5507) \end{array}$ 0.918   1.4248

20. Y $= \begin{array}{c} 458.989 \\ (37.2993) \end{array} + \begin{array}{c} 0.1773 \sum_{i=0}^{t-1} Ifi \\ (15.7332) \end{array}$ 0.947   0.8071

21. Y5s $= \begin{array}{c} 39.2400 \\ (-2.2064) \end{array} + \begin{array}{c} 0.4776Y \\ (16.9540) \end{array}$ 0.954   1.0363

22. Ifg $+ \begin{array}{c} 3.2268 \\ (1.1249) \end{array} + \begin{array}{c} 0.1820Rn \\ (6.3318) \end{array}$ 0.741   0.5439

B.   Identities (13)

1.   M $=$ C + I + G + X + mfs − Y − Xfs

2.   Mc $=$ M − Mk − Mig − Mos − Mfs

3.   Rn $=$ Tc + Te + Toi + Tyg + Tb + Typ − Trp − Trg − Trxg − Trmg − Tsu

4.   S $=$ Sg + Sp + Sb + Sd + Snmb

5.   Sg $=$ Rn − G

6.   Sp $=$ Yd − C − Trg − Trmp

7.   X $=$ Xg + Xs

8.   If $=$ Ifg + Ifpr

132

9. $I = If + In$

10. $Yd = Yp - Typ$

11. $Yp = Yn - Tb - Tyg - Sb + Trp$

12. $Yn = Y + Xfs - Mfs - Sd - (Tc + Te + Toi) + Tsu$

13. $Ifpr = S - In - Ifg$

SELECTED BIBLIOGRAPHY

A. Books

Agarwala, A. N., and Singh, S. P., eds. The Economics of Underdevelopment.
    Fair Lawn, N. J.: Oxford Press, 1958.

Baumol, William J. Economic Theory and Operations Analysis. 2nd ed. Englewood
    Cliffs, N. J.: Prentice – Hall, 1965

Bauer, Peter. T. and Yamey, Basil S. The Economics of Underdeveloped Countries.
    Chicago: University of Chicago Press, 1962.

Bowers, David A., and Baird, Robert N. Elementary Mathematical Macroeconomics
    Englewood Cliffs, N. J.: Prentice – Hall, 1971.

Brewster, H., and Thomas, C. Y. The Dynamics of West Indian Economic Integra-
    tion. Kingston: Institute of Social and Economic Research, U.W.I
    1967.

Central Planning Unit. Economic Survey Jamaica, 1969. Kingston, Jamaica:
    Government Publication, 1969
    Economic Survey Jamaica, 1970. Kingston Jamaica: Government
_____   Publication, 1970.
    Economic Survey Jamaica, 1971. Kingston, Jamaica, 1971

Clark, Colin. The Conditions of Economic Progress. 2nd ed. London: Mac Millon
    Press, 1951

Department of Statistics, Jamaica. National Income and Product, 1968. Kingston
    Jamaica: Government Publication, 1968.
    National Income and Product, 1973. Kingston, Jamaica:
_____   Government Publication, 1973
    National Income and Product, 1974. Kingston, Jamaica: Governmen
_____   Publication, 1974.
    National Income and Product, 1975. Kingston, Jamaica, 1975.

Duesenberry, J. S. Income, Saving and the Theory of Consumer Behavior.
    Cambridge, Mass.: Harvard University Press, 1949.

Evans, Michael K. Macroeconomic Activity: Theory, Forecasting and Control.
    New York: Harper and Row Publishers, 1969.

Friedman, Milton A Theory of the Consumption Function. Princeton, N. J.:
    Princeton University Press, 1957.

Harrod, R. F. Towards a Dynamic Economics. New York: St. Martin's Press, 1948

Jeffreyson, Owen The Post War Economic Development of Jamaica. Kingston:
    Institute of Social and Economic Research, 1972.

Keiser, Norman F. Macroeconomics, Fiscal Policy and Economic Growth. New York
    John Wiley and Sons Ltd., 1964

Kindleberger, Charles P. Economic Development. 2nd ed. New York: McGraw –
    Hill Book Company, 1965.

Klein, Lawrence R., and Goldberger, A. S. An Econometric Model of the United States, 1929 - 1952. New York: Humanities Press, 1955.

Lewis, W. A. The Theory of Economics Growth. New York: Richard D. Irwin, 1955.

Morgan, T., Betz, G. W. and Choudhry, N. K. eds. Readings in Economic Development. Belmont, Calif.: Wadsworth Press, 1963.

National Planning Agency. Economic and Social Survey, Jamaica, 1973. Kingston, Jamaica: Government Publication, 1973.
_____ Economic and Social Survey, Jamaica, 1974. Kingston, Jamaica: Government Publication, 1974. .
_____ Economic and Social Survey, Jamaica, 1975. Kingston, Jamaica: Government Publication, 1975.

Novack, David E., and Lekachman, Robert, eds. Development and Society: The Dynamics of Economic Change. New York: St. Martin's Press, 1968.

Okun, B., and R.W. Richardson, eds. Studies in Economic Development. New York: Holt, 1961.

Rostow, W. W. The Stages of Economic Growth. New York: Cambridge Press 1960.

Samuelson, Paul A. Economics. 10th ed. New York: McGraw-Hill, 1976.

Shourie, A. The Relevance of Econometric Models For Medium and Longer-Term Projections and Policy Prescriptions, International Bank for Reconstruction and Development (IRBD), Department of Economics, Work-Paper No. 75, May, 1970.

Solow, R. M. Growth Theory: An Exposition. New York: Oxford University Press, 1970.

United Nations. Studies in Long Term Projections for the World Economy: Aggregative Models. New York: United Nations, 1964.
_____ Problems of Long-Term Economic Projections. New York: Development Programming Techniques Series, No. 3, 1963.
_____ Trade Prospects and Capital Needs of Developing Countries. New York: United Nations Conference on Trade and Development (UNCTAD), 1968.

B. Articles

Abromovitz, M. "Resource and Output Trends in the United States since 1870." American Economic Review-Proceedings, May, 1956, 5 - 23.

Brown, T. M. "Habit Persistence and Consumer Behavior." Econometrica, Vol. 20 (July, 1952), 355-371.

Burton, H. J. "The Two-Gap Approach to Development: Comment" American Economic Review, June, 1969. 437 - 446.

Carter, Nicholas G. "A Macro–economic Model of Jamaica, 1959 – 1966."
Social and Economic Studies, June, 1970, 178 – 201.

Chenery, H. B., and Strout, A. M. "Foreign Assistance and Economic
Development." American Economic Review, September, 1966,
679 – 733.

Domar, E. D. "Capital Expansion, Rate of Growth and Employment."
Econometrica, April, 1946, 137 – 147.

Dutta, M., and Su, V. "An Economic Model of Puerto Rico." Review of
Economic Studies, XXXVl (July, 1969), 321.

Harris, Donald J. "Saving and Foreign Trade as Constraints in Economic Growth:
A Study of Jamaica." Social and Economic Studies, June, 1970,
147 – 177.

Heller, Walter "Fiscal Policies for Underdeveloped Countries." Agricultural
Taxation and Economic Development. Edited by H. Wald.
Cambridge, Mass.: Harvard University Law School, 1954.

Hirschman, Albert O. "How to Divest in Latin America and Why." Essays in
International Finance, No. 76, (November), Princeton University.

Kaldor, Nicholas. "A Model of Economic Growth." Economic Journal, December
1957, 591 –624.

Kennedy, Charles. "Keynesion Theory in an Open Economy." Social and Economic
Studies, No. 15 (March, 1966).

Klein, Lawrence R., and Schleicher, Stefan. "A Macro – Economic Model for
Mexico." Techniques of Model Building for Developing Economics:
Research Memorandum No. 91. Vienna: Institute for Advanced
Studies, 1975.

Lewis, W. A. "Economic Development with Unlimited Supplies of Labor." The
Manchester School, May, 1954, 139 – 191.

Manhertz, Huntley G. "An Exploratory Econometric Model of Jamaica," Social
and Economic Studies, June, 1971, 198 – 223.

Solow, Robert. "Technical Change and the Aggregate Production Function."
Review of Economics and Statistics, August, 1957, 312 –320
"Contribution to the Theory of Economic Growth." Quarterly
Journal of Economics, February, 1956, 65 – 94.
_____ "Technical Progress, Capital Formation and Economic Growth."
American Economic Review – Proceedings, May, 1962, 76 –86.

C. Miscellaneous

Consulate General of Jamaica, New Regulations for Bauxite Industry, May, 1974.
_____ Statement by the Prime Minister . . . On the Current Bauxite
Negotiations, May, 1974.
_____ Jamaica and Bauxite: the case for more Revenue, May, 1974.

136

INDEX

deepening, 43n.
formation, 4, 23, 89, 94
foreign, 30
imports, 11, 47-48
output ratio, 17-19,
    94-95, 110
as primary growth
    resource, 4
widening, 43n.
Capital Goods imports, 112
as intermediate goods, 48
proportion of total, 48
Capital intensive, 66
Carter, Nicholas, G., 6,
    7n., 8, 39n., 41n.,
    42n., 47n., 54n.,
    55, 56n., 57n.
Caribbean Development Bank,
    64-65
Central Planning Unit,
    55n., 58n.
Chenery, H.B., 22n.
China, 113
Choice, relationship to
    economics, 1
Choudhry, N.K., 108n.
Clarke, Colin, 108n.
Coefficient of determi-
    nation, 36-38
Coefficients, structural,
    110
Cold war, thawing and
    development, 120
Comparative advantage, 117
Compound growth rate, 30,
    32, 89
Constant return to scale,
    20
Construction, loss of
    vitality, 32-33
Consul General of Jamaica,
    59n.
Consumer, imports, 45-47
Consumption, 3
function, 34, 39-41
government, 41-42, 92

permanent income and, 40
personal, 26, 28, 39-41,
    93, 98, 104
Correlation, coefficient,
    84-85
between predicted and
    observed, 85-86
Custom duties, 12

D

Declining Secular trend, of
    Jamaican economy, 107
Department of Statistics,
    Jamaica, 61n., 63n.,
    77n., 79n., 86n.
Depreciation, 76-77
Demonstration effect, 3,
    13, 72
Development, Programming
    techniques, 4-5n.
Direct Taxes, 12-13
and business, 58-59
Diseconomies, 65
external, 72
Dissaving, 70
Domar, E.D., 17n.
Double log, 42n.
Duesenberry, J.S., 109
Durbin-Watson statistic,
    36-38
Dutta, M., 37n., 64n.

E

Economic model, of the
    United States, 6n.
for medium and longer
    term projections, 7n.
Economic development, 16-17,
    114
as economic growth, 16-17
compared with growth,
    16-17

139

net revenue, function of, 42

economic activity, function of, 42

Government investment, 79–80, 84, 92

Government revenue, 11–12, 29, 93, 104, 106

and development, 104

Government saving, 73–74, 104

Government sector, 24–25, 29, 94, 96, 111

Great Depression, 119

Gross Domestic Product, 30, 73, 90–93, 97, 100, 103–104, 106

Growth, a formula for, 18, historical trend of, 88–94

natural rate of, 18–19

steady state, 18

warranted rate of, 18

H

Harris, Donald J., 6, 45, 48n., 48, 51n., 54n., 56n., 57n., 58n., 61n., 77, 77n., 84n.

Harrod, E.F., 17, 19n.

Heller, Walter, 110n.

Hirschman, Albert O., 30n.

Historical growth rate, 15, 30, 98, 115

Hurricanes, 62, 64

I

Identities, 25–26

Import-export gap, 22, 30

Import substitution, 88, 101, 109

value to development, 112, 119

Imports, as endogenous variable, 29

and development, 119

Income effect, 60

Income, from government enterprises, 56–57, 75

Incremental, business taxes, 99

excise taxes, 99

custom taxes, 100

subsidies, 100

Incremental capital, 10

output ratio, 18–19 94–95

and growth, 94–95

Indirect taxes, 12, 53–56, 93, 104, 106

Industries:

Primary, 3, 107–108

Secondary, 3, 107–108

Tertiary, 3, 108

Industrial Incentive laws, 13, 66

Industrial sector, as function of gross domestic product, 29

and growth, 14

Inflation:

cost push, 3

demand pull, 3

through acceleration principle, 19

and progressive taxes, 59–60

Inter-American Development Bank, 64

Intermediate goods, 112

and industrial sector, 48

International Bank for Reconstruction and Development (IBRD) 7n.

International Monetary Fund (IMF), 116

143

exogenous factor, 100
government saving as, 74
personal saving as, 72
Richardson, R.W., 108n.
Rostow, W.W., 17n., 108n.

S

Samuelson, Paul A.,
    53n., 118n.
Saving, components of, 13,
    25
  personal, 3, 13-14, 70-72
    91, 93
  business, 91
  as residuals of consump-
    tion, 70-72
  foreign, 99, 101
  gross, 98
  ratio, 94-95, 108
Saving-Investment gap,
    11, 22n., 51, 78,
    99-100
Saving and Investment:
  local and growth, 111-112
  foreign, complimentary to
    growth, 112
Scarcity, relationship to
    economics, 1
Scheicher, Stefan, 64
Secondary industries, 3
  problems with, 107-108
Sectorial performance, 31-33
Shourie, A., 7n.
Simulation process, 79
Singh, S.P., 108n.
Solow, Robert, 20n., 110n.,
    111n.
Standard deviation, 84-85
Statistic, to, 36-38
  Dunbin-Watson, 36-38
Statistical estimation,
    36-38
Steady State growth, 18
Stochastic, equations, 70
  relationship, 37

Strout, A.M., 22
Su, V., 37n., 64n.
Subsidies, 13, 65-67
  as being negative to
    growth, 65-66
Substitution, of capital
    for labor, 19
  effect, 60
Supply capacity, 18

T

Tax, evasion, 58
  holidays, 12, 58, 66, 63
  reform, 58
Taxes, bauxite, 12, 58
  and capital formation,
    111
  custom, 53-55, 100
  Direct, 57-61, 91
  excise, 55, 99
  Indirect, 91
  pay as you earn ((PAYE),
    59
  personal income, 12,
    59-61, 91, 99
  progressive, 59
Technology, 110
  disembodied, 20
  embodied, 20
Ten year plan, 91-98
Terms of trade, 3
Tertiary industries, 3
  inadequate development
    of, 108
  instability of, 108
Third World countries,
    119-120
Thomas, C.Y., 65n.
Tourism, 3, 44, 47
  permanent income from, 13
  as core of service sector,
    108
Trade gap, 30, 88, 101
  financing, 30

146

ABOUT THE AUTHOR

Dr. Hugh N. Dawes graduated with Honors from the school of agriculture and general sciences at Twickenham Park, Jamaica, and served with the Jamaica government in different capacities. He obtained his Bachelor's degree from Cornell University and then went on to do his M.P.A. (Finance), M.A. and Ph.D. (Economics) degrees from New York University. He is currently a professor in economics with the City University of New York.